DISCOVERING THE BIBLE

THE RESURRECTION
of
JESUS

and other New Testament stories

RETOLD BY *Victoria Parker*

❖

CONSULTANT *Janet Dyson*

DISCOVERING THE BIBLE

THE RESURRECTION
of
JESUS

and other New Testament stories

RETOLD BY *Victoria Parker* ❖ CONSULTANT *Janet Dyson*

LORENZ BOOKS

Contents

First published in 2000 by Lorenz Books
© Anness Publishing Limited 2000
Lorenz Books is an imprint of
Anness Publishing Limited
Hermes House
88-89 Blackfriars Road
London SE1 8HA
This edition distributed in Canada by
Raincoast Books
8680 Cambie Street
Vancouver
British Columbia V6P 6M9

Publisher: Joanna Lorenz
Managing Editor: Gilly Cameron Cooper
Senior Editor: Lisa Miles

Produced by Miles Kelly Publishing Limited
Publishing Director: Jim Miles
Editorial Director: Paula Borton
Art Director: Clare Sleven
Project Editor: Neil de Cort
Editorial Assistant: Simon Nevill
Designer: Jill Mumford
Information Author: Kamini Khanduri
Artwork Commissioning: Suzanne Grant and Lynne French
Picture Research: Lesley Cartlidge and Libbe Mella,
Kate Miles and Janice Bracken
Copy Editing: AD Publishing Services
Indexing: Janet De Saulles
Design Consultant and Cover Design: Sarah Ponder
Education Consultant: Janet Dyson

PHOTOGRAPHIC CREDITS
Page 6, (BL), J.C. Tordai/The Hutchison Library; 13, (BL),
Gianni Dagli Orti/CORBIS; 25, (BR), Richard T.
Nowitz/CORBIS; 31 (BR), AFP/CORBIS; 39 (BL), Richard T.
Nowitz/CORBIS; 43 (BC), Dave Bartruff/CORBIS; 48 (BL),
Richard T. Nowitz/CORBIS; 50 (BR) Richard Hamilton
Smith/CORBIS; 51 (BL) Richard T. Nowitz/CORBIS; 57 (BC)
Arte & Immagini srl/CORBIS; 58 (BL) John Hatt/The
Hutchison Library; (BR) J.C. Tordai/The Hutchison Library;
59 (TL) The Hutchison Library; (TR) David Clilverd/The
Hutchison Library; (BL) The Hutchison Library; (BR) H.R.
Dörig/The Hutchison Library.
All other images from the Miles Kelly Archive
The Publishers would like to thank the following artists who
have contributed to this book:
Studio Galante (Virgil Pomfret Agency)

L.R. Galante   Manuela Cappon
Alessandro Menchi   Francesco Spadoni
                    Also
Sally Holmes   Terry Riley   Sue Stitt
Rob Sheffield   Mike Saunders   John James
Vanessa Card   Andrew Robinson   (Temple Rogers)
Maps by Martin Sanders
Printed and bound in Singapore
1 3 5 7 9 10 8 6 4 2

Introduction

HERE you can read about Jesus's last days on earth, from His arrival in Jerusalem to His betrayal by Judas which led to His arrest, trial and death. It ends with the story of His miraculous resurrection and His ascension to heaven, where He was reunited with God His Father.

Via Dolorosa
This carving shows Jesus on the way to Golgotha, just outside Jerusalem. It is situated on the Via Dolorosa, the "Way of Sorrow" in Jerusalem, along the route Jesus would have taken. It shows Simon of Cyrene helping Jesus with His cross.

The story begins with Jesus's last visit to Jerusalem. Jesus Himself was already aware that His entry into the city would lead to a final confrontation with the authorities, finishing with His own death. He told His disciples exactly what would happen, but they found it hard to believe His words. The visit took place during Passover time, so the streets were crowded with thousands of pilgrims. Instead of slipping in unnoticed, Jesus made a dramatic entry, riding on a donkey. This was interpreted as a fulfilment of the prophecy that the Messiah would enter Jerusalem on a donkey.

On His arrival in the city, Jesus immediately threw out of the temple the traders who were making money out of the pilgrims and increasing the profits of the corrupt temple officials. During the days that followed, Jesus preached in the temple area, while the religious leaders did their best to trick Him into incriminating Himself with statements of blasphemy, speaking against God. As the conflict escalated, the Jewish elders grew more determined to remove this troublemaker once and for all.

At the end of Passover week, Jesus held a farewell meal for His disciples. During this Last Supper, He gave some final instructions to His closest followers, and also revealed that He knew there was a traitor in their midst. After the meal, Jesus went to pray in the Garden of Gethsemane. He begged God to spare Him from His suffering and God sent an angel to give Him strength. Shortly after this, Jesus was arrested. The disciple Judas had betrayed Him to the Jewish elders, and had led them to the garden, showing them who Jesus was with a kiss.

Immediately after His arrest, Jesus was tried by the Jewish court, the Sanhedrin, and found guilty of blasphemy. Under Jewish law, blasphemy was punishable by death. At this time, though, only the Roman governor could pass the death sentence. Under Roman law,

Mount of Olives
In the hours before Jesus was arrested, He went to the Mount of Olives, shown here. He often went to the Garden of Gethsemane, which was on the Mount, to find peace from the bustle of Jerusalem itself.

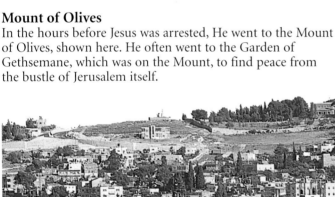

the charge of blasphemy was not even recognized. Because the Jewish leaders wanted Jesus dead, they brought Him before the Roman governor, Pontius Pilate, on a charge of treason. Although Pilate could find no case against Jesus, he bowed to public pressure and condemned Him to death by crucifixion.

Before the crucifixion took place, Jesus was savagely beaten and cruelly mocked by the Roman guards. The crucifixion itself involved a slow and very painful death. Throughout His ordeal, Jesus prayed to God to give Him the strength to bear the pain. One of the two thieves crucified alongside Jesus was impressed by His words of forgiveness and concern for others, even during His dreadful suffering. When Jesus died with a final cry of "It is finished", His body was taken down from the cross and buried in a nearby tomb.

According to the Bible, Jesus's tomb was found to be empty on the Sunday morning after His crucifixion. It was a group of women who made the discovery and, shortly afterwards, one of them, Mary Magdalene saw Christ alive again. For some weeks after this, Jesus made several appearances to His disciples, both in Galilee and Jerusalem. When He had convinced them that He had overcome death, and assured them that He would continue to help them even when He was no longer physically present, He departed, leaving them to carry on His work. The disciples watched in amazement as their master ascended to heaven, to return to His Father.

Throughout these stories we can see Jesus's suffering, and His strength in the face of that suffering. Jesus accepted His death and never denied God. Christians believe that when Jesus died, He took upon Himself the sins of everyone, so that anyone could be forgiven by God and live with Him for ever. They believe that Jesus accepted the pain of death to show, by His resurrection, that God and His love are not defeated by death. Christians try to follow Jesus's example, living their lives according to God's purpose of saving the world through love.

The other important aspect is Jesus's miraculous resurrection. The Christian idea of resurrection was different from the beliefs of other religions at the time. Christians thought of the body as being resurrected, and of it being transformed so that it was suitable for the eternal life to follow. The Greeks were different. They thought of the body as a hindrance to true life and believed that after death, the soul would leave the body behind entirely. Their concept of life after death was in terms of a soul that never died. The Jews believed in resurrection, but thought it would be with the same body.

The resurrection has been of central importance to the Christian faith since the earliest preaching began. Right from the start, Christians believed that Jesus had risen from the dead, and that they too would rise after death to be with God eternally. Jesus said, "I am the resurrection and the life; he who believes in me, though he die, yet shall he live".

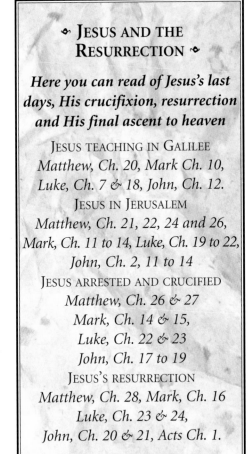

> ❧ **JESUS AND THE RESURRECTION** ❧
>
> *Here you can read of Jesus's last days, His crucifixion, resurrection and His final ascent to heaven*
>
> JESUS TEACHING IN GALILEE
> *Matthew, Ch. 20, Mark Ch. 10, Luke, Ch. 7 & 18, John, Ch. 12.*
> JESUS IN JERUSALEM
> *Matthew, Ch. 21, 22, 24 and 26, Mark, Ch. 11 to 14, Luke, Ch. 19 to 22, John, Ch. 2, 11 to 14*
> JESUS ARRESTED AND CRUCIFIED
> *Matthew, Ch. 26 & 27*
> *Mark, Ch. 14 & 15,*
> *Luke, Ch. 22 & 23*
> *John, Ch. 17 to 19*
> JESUS'S RESURRECTION
> *Matthew, Ch. 28, Mark, Ch. 16*
> *Luke, Ch. 23 & 24,*
> *John, Ch. 20 & 21, Acts Ch. 1.*

Jesus taken from the cross
After He died, Jesus was taken down from the cross by Joseph of Arimathea, seen here with Mary Magdalene, and Mary, mother of James and John. Joseph was a member of the Sanhedrin, the ruling Jewish council who wanted Jesus dead, although he had voted against Jesus's death. The Bible tells us that Joseph was a secret disciple of Jesus. Joseph was wealthy, so he was able to provide rich linen in which to wrap Jesus's body. He also had his own tomb carved out of the rock, and it was in this tomb that Jesus was buried.

Jesus in Jerusalem

THE CITY OF JERUSALEM, where Jesus was tried and crucified, was, even at this time, a very important city. Its history can be traced back to at least 3000 years before the birth of Jesus, and today it is considered sacred not only to Christians, but to followers of Judaism and Islam as well. The first part of its name means "foundation". The second part, *salem*, probably originally referred to Shalem, a Canaanite god or goddess. The Canaanites were the race of people that lived in this area before the Israelites arrived. So the original meaning of the name was probably "foundation of Shalem". Over the years, though, the second part of the name probably came to be associated, in the minds of the Jewish people living there, with the Jewish word *salom*, meaning peace.

Since the start of His ministry, Jesus had known that He would meet His death in Jerusalem. He had told His disciples many times that this would be the case, but they had never entirely believed him. Jesus wanted to make sure that as many people as possible heard and understood His message, so His last days in Jerusalem are full of symbols that the people could have picked up on, and that would give them clues as to His mission.

Jesus deliberately made His final trip to Jerusalem at the time of the Jewish festival of Passover. During this feast the Jews remember the events that took place when their ancestors were slaves in Egypt. Before the pharaoh of Egypt would release the Israelites from slavery, God, through Moses, had inflicted nine plagues upon the pharaoh and his country. In the tenth and final plague God killed all the first-born children and animals in Egypt. However, He "passed-over" the houses of the Israelites who had followed special instructions for the first Passover meal given to them by God through Moses.

Death of Christ
The death and the resurrection of Jesus are the most important things for the Christian faith. Christ's suffering is sometimes used symbolically, such as in this image of a peasant praying before Christ. The peasant, dressed as he is, could not have been present for the real crucifixion. He is praying to the forgiving spirit of Jesus.

When Jesus enters Jerusalem during Passover week, not only is the city more crowded than usual because of the all the pilgrims who have come to the holy city to celebrate, but these people are already thinking about death and being saved by God, as it is the reason that many of them are in Jerusalem.

Jesus made a highly symbolic entry into the holy city. The Old Testament tells how a Messiah would come and save the Jewish people. This Messiah, the Bible says, would enter Jerusalem on a donkey. Jesus knew exactly what message He was giving the people. Throughout His ministry, Jesus had told only His disciples that He was the Messiah, and He had told them not to tell anyone. At this stage, though, He is arriving in Jerusalem to fulfil the role on earth that God gave Him and can He tell everyone that He is the Messiah.

Soon after entering Jerusalem, Jesus went to the temple and again fulfilled Old Testament prophecies by clearing the traders from it, as He had done once before. By making His anger and displeasure publicly very clear, Jesus was making known His anger at the religious authorities of the time, the Sadducees and the Pharisees, for allowing, and sometimes encouraging, the traders and the money-changers into the grounds of the temple.

Jesus's time in Jerusalem is traced on this map. The Bible tells us that He was staying in Bethany, and came every morning of Passover week to the temple to teach the people. You can see the site of the Passover meal that Jesus took with His disciples, the Last Supper, before the group followed Jesus out to the Garden of Gethsemane for Jesus to pray. In the Garden, Jesus was betrayed, as He knew He would be, by Judas to the authorities. Jesus was arrested and taken for an unofficial trial at the house of Annas, the former High Priest. Jesus was then taken to the house of Caiaphas, the high priest, where He was tried for blasphemy, speaking against God, by the whole Sanhedrin, the Jewish council. The punishment under Jewish law for this crime was death, but the Jewish authorities could not order Jesus's execution, only the Roman governor could do that. The elders had a problem, though. They knew that Pontius Pilate, the Roman governor, would not recognise a charge of blasphemy as he was not concerned with the Jewish religion. In order to get Jesus executed, they changed the charge, they told Pilate that Jesus was trying to stir people up to fight against the Romans. The elders hoped that the governor would not be able to ignore a charge of this sort. Even though Pilate could find no charge on which he could find Jesus guilty, the elders had done such a good job of stirring up hate among the people of Jerusalem that Pilate eventually bowed under the pressure from the public and allowed Jesus to be led away. Jesus was taken to Golgotha, outside the city walls, where the Romans crucified Him.

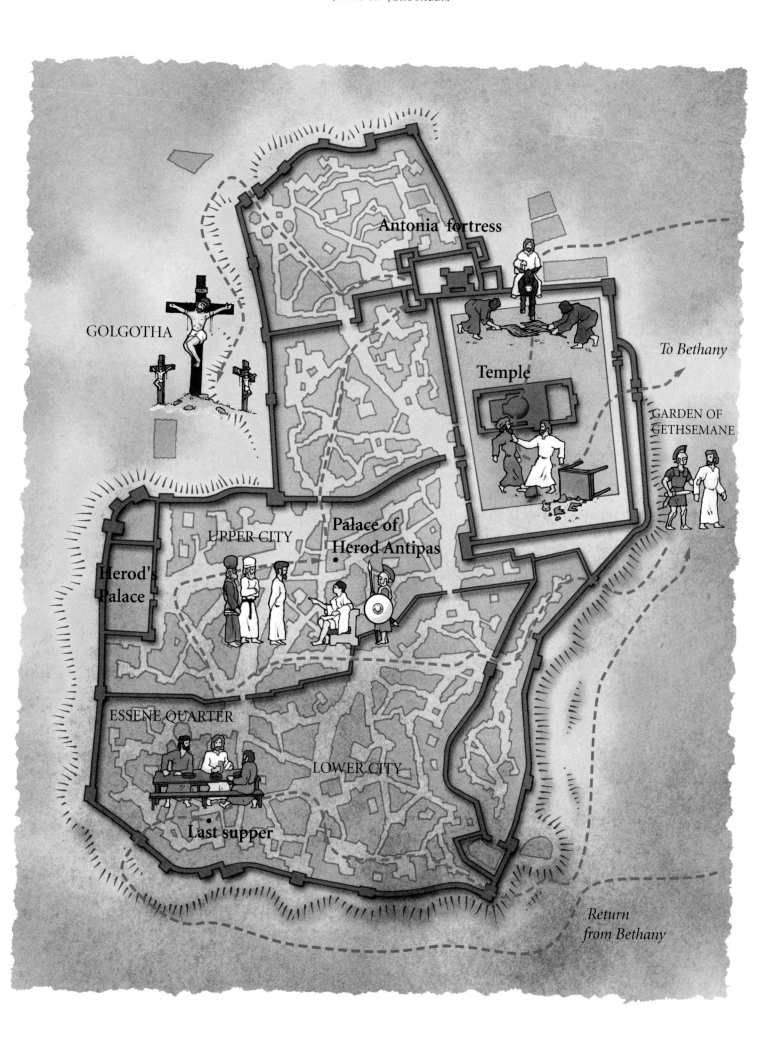

GOLGOTHA

Antonia fortress

Temple

To Bethany

GARDEN OF
GETHSEMANE

UPPER CITY

Palace of
Herod Antipas

Herod's
Palace

ESSENE QUARTER

LOWER CITY

Last supper

Return
from Bethany

Jesus Turns for Jerusalem

THE 12 disciples had been travelling around Judea for three years. Every day they had walked for hours, relying on the goodness of strangers to feed and shelter them. Every day, they had dealt with the masses of pushing, shouting people who had come to see Jesus. The disciples had listened to hundreds of people pour out their problems. They had given the downcast men and women new hope by preaching Jesus's message of God's kingdom. They had seen people with terrible illnesses and diseases, taking many to Jesus for healing and healing others themselves. They had stood up against the anger of the religious authorities, who insisted that Jesus was a wicked hoaxer

leading the people into sin. They had faced the violent mobs who came to stop Jesus and His disciples by force. In private, the disciples had struggled to understand as Jesus explained His teachings. Each one of them had carried in His heart the great secret Jesus had told them: that He was the Messiah, God's chosen one, the one the prophets said long ago would be sent to save the world from its sins.

It was hard work, and one night's sleep was never enough. However, the disciples were dedicated. They believed wholeheartedly in Jesus and were determined to follow Him, no matter how difficult it was.

One morning, Jesus was already up and saying His prayers. The disciples hurried to join Him. Then they sat back and waited for Jesus's instructions. Jesus's words were strange and worrying.

"It is time for me to go to Jerusalem," He explained.

Jesus looked around and saw both excitement and worry in the disciples' faces. He had told His 12 helpers

❧ ABOUT THE STORY ❧

Jesus had probably been to Jerusalem several times during His three-year ministry. He knew that this time would be different. The opposition had grown to fever pitch. He must have been afraid, because He knew it would be painful. He also knew that this was why He had come into the world. So Jesus set out to do God's will, because He knew that God's will was the best for Him, and for everyone.

The Messiah
In the Old Testament, it is prophesied that the Messiah will come to save the Jewish people. In the New Testament, Jesus is described as the Messiah, come to save mankind. The word "messiah" comes from the Hebrew word meaning "anointed one". The Greek word for anointing, "christos", is the origin of Jesus's title, "Christ".

long ago that they were working their way towards Jerusalem, and the disciples were well aware of the dangers that lay ahead there. Although the Romans were governing Judea, the elders in Jerusalem had great power and they wanted Jesus out of the way. Once Jesus was in the capital city, it would be much easier for the priests, scribes and Pharisees to get their hands on Him.

Jesus looked at His anxious friends and smiled sadly.

"I've already told you what will happen to me there," He said, "but I know that none of you have been able to believe it. Yet my words are true. In Jerusalem, everything that the ancient prophets said would happen to the Son of Man will finally come to pass. I will be handed over to the chief priests and scribes. They will condemn me to death and give me to my enemies to be mocked and tortured. Finally, I will be put to death by crucifixion and three days later, I will be raised up to life again."

The disciples all began to speak at once, clamouring and questioning and protesting. Jesus held up His hand for silence. As the twelve men brooded, their eyes downcast and their minds troubled, the mother of James and John came hurrying up and knelt before Jesus.

> **Grant us to sit, one at your right hand and one at your left, in your glory.**

"Lord," she said. "Please let my two sons sit beside you in your kingdom – one at your right hand, the other at your left."

Jesus's voice was low and firm.

"Only my Father can grant that," He replied. "However, I can tell you that anyone who would be great in my Father's kingdom must be a humble servant to others here on earth. I myself came here to serve others – not to have others serve me – and to give up my own life to save the lives of many."

Jesus's journey to Jerusalem
During His ministry in Galilee, Jesus visited Jerusalem several times. The journey that He made from Capernaum to Jerusalem was a long one, nearly 160km on foot.

Brooch
The Romans wore many types of jewellery including brooches like this one. Brooches were often ornate and were worn by both men and women. They had safety pins on the back and were used to fasten clothes, such as cloaks, at the shoulder.

Christian Symbol
The cross is a sign of Christianity because it represents the cross on which Jesus was crucified. Some Christians wear a cross, usually around the neck, as a sign of their commitment to Jesus.

Jesus is Anointed

ON His way to Jerusalem, Jesus stopped at the little town of Bethany to stay with His close friends, Mary, Martha and Lazarus.

The two sisters and their brother were overjoyed to see Jesus. They had every faith in His teachings and loved Him dearly, not least because Lazarus owed his life to Jesus. Once, after a sudden illness, Mary and Martha's brother had died. Four days later, Jesus had arrived and brought Lazarus walking out of his tomb alive and well.

Now the little family welcomed Jesus with open arms, each providing the best hospitality they could. Martha rushed around in the kitchen, preparing a delicious meal. Lazarus was the perfect host, keeping all his guests entertained and happy while they sat waiting at the table. Mary saw how weary the travellers were from their journeying, and slipped away to fetch something to soothe and refresh Jesus. She decided on a tiny bottle of scent she had been saving – the most rare and expensive perfume that money could buy. Mary didn't give Jesus just a few dabs of it. Instead, she cracked open the precious alabaster flask and let every last drop of the cool, beautiful perfume trickle over His hot, tired skin.

Several of the disciples leapt to their feet in shock at the very extravagant gesture.

"What are you doing, woman?" cried Judas Iscariot, totally appalled. "You would have been better off selling that perfume and giving all the money to the poor!"

"Leave Mary alone," Jesus scolded. "You will always have poor people to show generosity to, but you will not always have me. By anointing me with this beautiful perfume, Mary has in fact prepared my body for burial."

> " *'In pouring this ointment on my body she has done it to prepare me for burial.'* "

The disciples looked at each other in puzzlement and began to whisper about what Jesus could mean by speaking of burials and of not always being with them. Jesus Himself stayed silent, wrapped up in memories of another time, not too long before, when a woman had shown Him a similar kindness.

Once, when He had been dining at a Pharisee's house, a woman He had never met before had hurried to see Him. The woman had been a terrible sinner all her life, but she had heard Jesus speak of love and repentance, and she had felt something inside her change. From then on, all she had truly wanted was to be forgiven and to be able to make a new start.

The woman had sat behind Jesus and cried. Her tears had fallen on His feet, dusty from the road, and had washed them clean. She had dried Jesus's wet feet with her hair and tenderly kissed them. She opened up an expensive bottle of perfume that she had brought with her especially, and scented His skin.

Jesus had been very touched by the woman's kindness, which was quite the opposite of His host's. The Pharisee hadn't gone to any trouble at all to make Jesus feel welcome. When he had seen that Jesus was allowing the sinning woman to touch Him, the Pharisee had practically turned up his nose and shifted his seat further away in disgust.

At this, Jesus had told His host a story. "Two men owed money to a moneylender," He had said. "One owed a large amount and the other owed a small amount. Neither man was able to repay what he had borrowed, and the moneylender let them both off their debts. Which man would feel more grateful?"

"The one who owed more money," the Pharisee had replied.

"Exactly," Jesus had agreed. "Compare yourself with this sinning woman. You gave me no water to wash with, but this woman has washed my feet with her tears. You gave me no towel to dry them, but she has dried them with her hair. You gave me no kiss of greeting, but she has covered my feet with kisses. You gave me no scent to freshen up with, but this woman

has brought me expensive perfume. I can tell you that all her sins are forgiven, and so she shows me much love."

The other guests had murmured angrily, "Who does this man think He is, to say that He can forgive sins?"

But Jesus hadn't taken any notice of the offended guests' remarks. Instead, He had simply turned to the young woman and smiled. "Your faith has saved you," He had said, gently. "Go in peace."

Alabaster
The perfume bottle in the story is made from a translucent stone called alabaster. Alabaster is very soft and easy to carve, this Turkish relief is made of alabaster. Only expensive perfumes would have been kept in alabaster bottles. Everyday perfumes were kept in pottery jars.

Precious perfume
Perfumes were made from many kinds of plants, herbs and spices and were imported into Palestine from countries such as India and Egypt. When Mary anoints Jesus with her best perfume, she is honouring Him as a special guest and showing her devotion to Him.

❖ ABOUT THE STORY ❖
The Pharisees thought that by keeping all their religious ceremonies they would be good enough to please God. They forgot that sometimes there was anger, hatred and greed in their hearts. That was a sin against God. This woman knew she had sinned and so said sorry. She could be forgiven. People who did not think they had done wrong could not please God. They had to say sorry for their sins, too.

The First Palm Sunday

IT was the week before the great feast of the Passover. Jews from all over Judea were hurrying to Jerusalem for the celebrations, and the authorities were desperate to know whether Jesus would dare visit the temple with all the other worshippers. The chief priests and scribes and Pharisees had given out strict orders that if anyone knew where the "trouble-making" preacher was, they should let them know immediately, so they could arrest Him.

Jesus and His disciples were at Bethany with Mary, Martha and Lazarus. By the time the authorities heard, hundreds of people had left Jerusalem to see Jesus.

The Jewish elders were furious. They couldn't possibly seize Him in the middle of His supporters. Instead, the chief priests and scribes and Pharisees gathered their spies to them once again.

"We'll have to wait and see if Jesus comes to Jerusalem for Passover," they hissed. "Keep a sharp eye out. He'll probably try to mingle unnoticed among the crowds."

They needn't have gone to such trouble. The Sunday before Passover, Jesus and His disciples set off quite openly for Jerusalem, surrounded by a cheering crowd. The disciples sang Jesus's praises aloud as they accompanied their master to Beth-page, which lay close to the capital city on the Mount of Olives.

"Go into the village," Jesus instructed two of His disciples. "There you will find a donkey tethered to a doorway. Untie it and bring it to me. If anyone asks what you're doing, just say that the Lord needs it."

The men hurried off and, sure enough, they found the donkey, just as Jesus had said. As soon as the owners found out who it was that wanted to borrow the animal, they threw their robes on its back for a saddle and gladly brought it to Jesus themselves.

"Be careful though," the owners told Jesus. "He might be quite wild. No one has sat on him before."

When Jesus mounted the donkey, it stood still and calm and obedient. It was on the gentle, grey animal's back that Jesus set off again, heading for the holy city.

At this, a new wave of excitement rippled through the crowd accompanying Jesus. The ancient prophets had foretold that the Messiah would one day enter Jerusalem on a donkey! This must be Him, they thought.

Hundreds of men, women and children came running out to greet Jesus, cheering excitedly. Some took off their robes and spread them out over the road, while others paved the way with broad palm leaves and flowers.

"Hosanna!" they shouted. "Blessed is He who comes in the name of the Lord! Hosanna in the highest!"

All the way to Jerusalem, people poured out to welcome Jesus. When Jesus saw the city itself, He began to weep.

> " *So they took branches of palm trees and went out to meet Him.* "

"Oh Jerusalem!" He murmured. "Though you greet me now, you will fail to believe that God has come to you. Because of that, you will be utterly destroyed."

Everyone was far too excited to notice Jesus's sorrow, as the joyful procession wound its way around the city.

JESUS ENTERED JERUSALEM LIKE A VICTORIOUS KING. BUT THE VICTORY STILL HAD TO BE WON. HE WOULD DEFEAT SIN AND HIS DEATH ON THE CROSS WHEN HE ROSE FROM THE DEAD.

Palm Sunday
Here is Jesus on the donkey, making His way to Jerusalem. The people lining the route are laying palm leaves on the ground in front of Him. Many churches celebrate Palm Sunday today with processions in which branches of palms are carried.

"Hosanna to the son of David!" they cried. "Blessed is the King who comes in the name of the Lord! Hosanna in the highest!"

"This is outrageous!" the purple-faced Pharisees yelled at Jesus. "These people think that you're the Messiah! Tell them to stop at once!"

"Even if they were silent," Jesus replied, "the very stones would cry out."

Passover meal
Jesus entered Jerusalem in the week before the great Jewish feast of the Passover. People now date the Christian Easter celebration in the same way the Jews decide the date of Passover, based on the Jewish cycle of the moon.

The graceful palm
A palm is a tall tree with a straight, narrow trunk and a cluster of huge feathery leaves at the top. Palm leaves were a symbol of grace and victory. They were laid down in front of Jesus as a mark of respect.

> ❖ **ABOUT THE STORY** ❖
> *King David and his family had ridden on donkeys (or mules) in Old Testament times. There was an Old Testament prophecy that said the Messiah would enter Jerusalem like this. So Jesus was showing that He had come to fulfil the prophecies and that He claimed to be David's successor.*
>
> *It was a powerful visual message. Some people, though, like the Sadducees, did not believe the fulfillment of the prophecy before their eyes.*

Jesus in the Temple

JESUS was horrified to find that the great temple of Jerusalem was being used as a market place. Money changers were transferring foreign coins into Jewish shekels and making handsome profits for themselves. Stallholders were selling sacrificial animals to the pilgrims at ridiculously high prices. Instead of the reverential silence Jesus expected, His ears throbbed with the buzz of bartering, the lowing of livestock, the shouting of friends and everyday chit-chat.

Jesus had seen the temple dishonoured in this way a couple of years ago. With a furious cry of, "Take these things away! You will not make my Father's house into a business place!" Jesus had driven all the traders out by force. It had not taken them long to return.

Now Jesus exploded with even greater anger.

"The temple should be a house of prayer for all the nations of the world!" He roared. "You have made it into a den of thieves!"

Jesus went through the courtyards like a whirlwind. He pushed over the money changers' tables, sending coins spilling on to the floor and cascading down the steps. He smashed open the bird cages, releasing doves into the air. He flung the livestock traders into the dusty streets, sending their cattle and sheep stampeding after them.

Finally, the temple was cleared. It didn't stay empty for long, though. Crowds of people soon flooded back in to see Jesus, packing the courtyard.

"Tell us about God's kingdom!" came the shouts. "What must we do to have our sins forgiven?"

Other voices cried out for healing.

As soon as Jesus began to speak, the temple fell silent as everyone concentrated on His every word.

Each evening through Passover week, Jesus would return to Bethany. Then, every morning, He would go straight back to the temple in Jerusalem. He would stand until nearly dusk, preaching His message of hope and salvation, and laying His hands on whoever was in need, making them well again.

When the Jewish elders saw the wonderful things Jesus did and heard the excited children crying out, "Hosanna to the Son of David!" they couldn't stand it. They came stomping right into the middle of the crowds and shook their staffs in Jesus's face.

"By whose permission are you teaching here?" the Jewish dignitaries raged. "Who has given you the authority to stir up the people like this?"

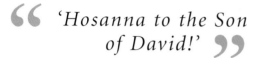

> ‘Hosanna to the Son
> of David!’

"Let me ask you a question, and if you can answer it, then I'll tell you," Jesus replied calmly. "Now, who gave my cousin John the right to baptize? Did God want him to do it or was it just the people?"

The Jewish elders scratched their heads.

"If we say God, Jesus will ask us why we didn't believe John's teachings," they argued. "However, if we say the people, the crowds here will probably stone us. For they believe that John was a true prophet from God."

"We don't know!" they spat, their faces like thunder.

USUALLY, PEOPLE GET ANGRY WHEN THEY HAVE BEEN HURT PERSONALLY. JESUS'S ACTION SHOWS THAT GOD FEELS ANGRY AND HURT WHEN PEOPLE DO NOT TAKE HIM AND HIS WORSHIP SERIOUSLY.

Temple traders
Roman traders in the temple are selling doves to be used as sacrifices to God. Jesus is angry when He sees this going on, as this sort of behaviour is wrong in a place of worship. To make matters worse, the traders are taking advantage of the pilgrims' faith by charging high prices for the birds.

They knew that they could not give either answer.

"Well, if you can't tell me that," replied Jesus, "then I can't tell you by what authority I say and do these things."

Once again, Jesus had managed to keep the hostile Jewish authorities at bay. However, they weren't about to give up and leave Him alone. For the chief priests, scribes and Pharisees, plotting Jesus's death had become their number one concern.

Pilgrims

People who travel to a holy place for religious reasons are called pilgrims. Many of Jesus's followers travelled long distances to see Him and listen to His teachings. These pilgrims are in Jerusalem during Passover week.

Weighing their wares

This bronze steelyard was hung by its upper hook and used by traders for weighing their goods. The object to be weighed was attached to the lower hook and the acorn-shaped weight was moved along the long arm until it balanced in a straight line.

❧ ABOUT THE STORY ❧

This story shows that Jesus was not always gentle, meek and mild. Here, He is like one of the Old Testament prophets calling down God's judgement on people. Jesus often taught about God's judgement, as well as about His love. He warned people who took God's love for granted that they could be in for a big shock when God shut them out of His kingdom. He does judge and He does forgive. Both truths are important.

The Wicked Tenants

BY Tuesday of Passover Week, everyone in Jerusalem knew Jesus was speaking out against the authorities.

"Once upon a time," Jesus preached, "a man planted a vineyard. When all the work was done, he had to leave for another country. So he brought in tenants to look after the vineyard.

"Time passed, and the owner sent a servant to bring back some of the first crop of grapes for him to sample. The servant returned empty-handed and covered in bruises. The tenants had refused to hand over any crops, and had beaten up the servant. The vineyard owner tried again. However, the second servant came back more severely wounded than the first. The third time the vineyard owner sent a servant, he didn't return at all. The tenants actually killed him.

"Still the vineyard owner didn't give up. He kept on sending servants. The tenants beat up some and murdered others, until there was only one man left: his own son, whom he loved dearly. Surely they will respect him, the vineyard owner thought. To his great sorrow and regret, the tenants butchered his son just like the others.

> ❝ *I will send my beloved son.* ❞

"Now, I will tell you what the vineyard owner will do next," Jesus announced to the crowds in the temple. "He will come and destroy the wicked tenants and give the vineyard to others who deserve it."

Everyone knew Jesus meant the tenants were the Jewish elders and the vineyard was the kingdom of God. The elders seethed to hear it.

❖ ABOUT THE STORY ❖

Jesus is not just telling this story against the religious leaders of His day. It includes their ancestors too. It is a sad story that sums up how people had treated God's servants for many centuries. The tenants are the leaders in every age. The servants are prophets who God sent to call people back to Himself. So often, these servants were ignored or got rid of. Soon, this generation of leaders will kill God's Son, Jesus.

Grapes and wine
This glass flask, made to look like a bunch of grapes, would have been used to hold wine. Grapes were very important in Roman times. Grown in vineyards, they were eaten as fresh fruit and dried as raisins. They were also pressed to make juice and wine. The Romans drank a great deal of wine, and wine-making was a well-established business during these times.

Jesus as the son
In this story, Jesus is using the death of the vineyard owner's son to symbolize His own death, as the son of God, at the hands of the Sadducees and Pharisees.

The Barren Fig Tree

ONE morning when Jesus was hurrying from Bethany to Jerusalem, His stomach began to rumble. He had left so early to get to the great temple to begin preaching and healing that He and His disciples had had no time for breakfast. So when Jesus caught sight of a fig tree growing by the roadside, He called a halt for a few seconds and went over to pick some of its juicy fruit for Himself and His companions to eat.

However, when Jesus drew closer to the tall, leafy tree, He was dismayed to find that there wasn't a single fig among the branches.

"May you never grow any fruit ever again!" He cried.

The disciples stood and watched open-mouthed as all at once its leaves faded to yellow, then crinkled to brown, then fluttered from the branches to the ground. The tree that had been alive and green just a few moments ago now stood bare and dry and withered.

> " *Jesus answered them, 'Have faith in God...'* "

The 12 men gasped. Even though they had witnessed Jesus perform many dramatic miracles, they had never seen Him use His powers except to help people in some way. In fact, whenever anyone had challenged Jesus to prove Himself by performing a miracle "just for show", He had always refused. Now all of a sudden He had destroyed a harmless tree.

"Why?" the stunned disciples spluttered.

"To show that if you only have faith in God, you will find that you can make anything happen," Jesus replied. "I tell you that when you pray, if you truly believe that God has heard you and will answer you, you will surely receive whatever you prayed for. Remember, always forgive others who do you wrong. For then, in turn, your Father in heaven will be able to forgive the things that you yourself do wrong."

Deep in thought, the disciples continued with Jesus on their way...

Picking figs
This picture shows a man picking ripe figs from a tree. Together with grapes and olives, figs were an important fruit. The common fig is mentioned more than fifty times in the Bible and the Hebrew language has four different words for "fig". Figs were eaten as fruit, pressed into fig-cakes and also used in medicine.

FAITH IS NOT LIKE KNOWLEDGE. IT CANNOT BE TESTED IN AN EXAM TO SEE HOW MUCH WE HAVE GOT. WE EITHER HAVE IT, OR WE DO NOT, BECAUSE FAITH IS SIMPLY TRUSTING GOD.

❖ ABOUT THE STORY ❖

This is a strange thing for Jesus to do – He did not usually destroy things. It was even harder to understand because it was not the right time of year for figs! Jesus is acting out a parable. God's people are meant to bear fruit – that is, to do what God wants. He is saying that the fig tree stands for God's people who have rejected Him and that they will wither away like the tree. Sure enough, in AD 70, the Romans destroyed Judea.

Jesus is Put to the Test

THE Jewish authorities were desperate. "There must be something we can do to stop this Jesus of Nazareth!" the highest Jewish officials discussed in secret. "We can't get rid of Him by force because He's always surrounded by adoring crowds. If we went to arrest Him and they turned on us, we'd be totally outnumbered.

"We've warned everyone that Jesus isn't even a prophet, let alone the Messiah, and we've told the people that He's turning them away from our true religion. They're so bewitched by Jesus that they're not taking any notice.

"We can stand in the middle of the temple and shout and yell and stamp our feet as much as we like. It doesn't seem to have the slightest effect on Jesus."

After a lot of scheming, the chief priests and scribes decided to try a different tack. They ordered their spies to go and mingle with Jesus's

supporters in the temple. They were told to try and lead Him into saying something that would break the law. The Jewish elders rubbed their hands with glee at the thought of finally catching Jesus out. Their enemy would soon be hauled in front of the Roman provincial governor for judgement and punishment – and the harsher the better!

"Teacher," the spies wheedled from among the temple crowds. "We know that you truly teach the way of God. He is the only leader you respect and the law of heaven is the only law you follow. So what should we do about earthly leaders and earthly laws? For instance, the Roman Emperor Caesar demands that we give him taxes. Should we pay this tribute or not?"

"Why are you putting me to the test?" Jesus said. He wasn't fooled for one second.

> " *Knowing their hypocrisy, He said to them, 'Why put me to the test?'* "

"Look at this coin," Jesus instructed, showing a piece of Roman money to the spies. "Whose head and inscription does it have on it?"

"Caesar's," the spies mumbled.

"Exactly," replied Jesus, flipping the coin at them. "So give to Caesar the things that belong to Caesar, and give to God the things that belong to God."

With his answer, Jesus had dashed the plans of the Jewish elders yet again. Despite their bitter frustration and disappointment, even they couldn't help but be awed by the wisdom of the carpenter's son from Nazareth.

❧ ABOUT THE STORY ❧

One of the big debates among the Jews of the 1st century AD was how they should regard the Romans who occupied their country. Some wanted to rebel and fight the Romans. Others accepted the invaders in order to make life easy. So this was a clever question. If Jesus sided with the Romans, He was a traitor to the Jews. If He sided with the Jews, He was a traitor to the Romans. He still got out of it!

The Roman battlefield
The taxes that Caesar demanded were used to run the empire. This included paying for the hated Roman army pictured here in a battle with barbarians.

Roman standard
The Roman standard was the ceremonial emblem, carried on a pole, by soldiers in the army. The Roman army was the most efficient in the world and the standard was a symbol of power and strength.

Jewish Elders Try a Trick

THE Sadducees tried to trip Jesus up and expose Him as a fraud. They thought up the trickiest question they could imagine and strode confidently to the temple to put it to Jesus.

"If a woman has been widowed seven times," the smug Sadducees asked Jesus, "which of the seven men she married will be her husband in the life after death?"

The Sadducees didn't know the answer to questions like these, so they had come to the conclusion that life after death couldn't exist. They still thought they were cleverer than everyone else for having come up with the questions at all.

Yet Jesus wasn't at all foxed.

"You know nothing of the scriptures or the power of God," He replied bluntly. "When people are raised from the dead, they are not married. They are like angels in heaven. As for life after death, haven't you read in the scriptures that God said, 'I am the God of Abraham and Isaac and Jacob'? As you know, He's not the God of the dead, He's the God of the living!"

After that, the stunned Sadducees didn't dare ask Jesus any more questions. The Pharisees did.

"What is the greatest of all of God's commandments?" they asked Jesus.

"To love God with all your heart and mind and soul," Jesus replied at once. "Second most important is to love your neighbour as you love yourself. All the other commandments rest on these two."

The Pharisees were dumbstruck. Jesus didn't just know the scriptures better than anyone else, he understood them better, too.

"Now let me ask you a question of my own," Jesus said. "If the Christ is the son of King David, how come in the scriptures David calls the Christ 'Lord'?"

Of course, the Pharisees didn't know the answer. And, as they stood gaping open-mouthed, they heard titters of laughter ripple through the temple crowds.

"This man is making us look like fools!" the chief priests, scribes, Sadducees and Pharisees raged in private. "We have to get rid of Him if it's the last thing we do!"

Jesus and the saints
This stone carving shows Jesus surrounded by symbolic representations of the saints, Matthew, Mark, Luke and John. These saints wrote the four Gospels, the books in the Bible that tell us about Jesus's life and teaching.

❖ ABOUT THE STORY ❖

The Sadducees only accepted the first five books of the Old Testament and they would not believe anything that was elsewhere in the Bible. They were very unpopular and acted in a very superior way. They loved intellectual arguments, which were of no help to people who wanted to know God better. They were not open to what God might say; they just wanted to prove Jesus was not one of them.

The Great Denunciation

THE trouble between Jesus and the Jewish authorities had reached boiling point. It was as if the temple itself was split into a battlefield, with the chief priests and scribes mustering their forces on one side, while Jesus roused His loyal troops on the other.

"The scribes and Pharisees follow in the footsteps of Moses," Jesus preached, in a loud clear voice. "So do as they say." He paused for a second, to make sure He had everyone's full attention. "However, make sure you don't do as they do, for they are hypocrites!"

The hundreds of listeners gasped as if with one voice.

Jesus's eyes sparkled with anger. His hair bristled with outrage. "Everything they do is for show!" He roared. "They recite long elaborate prayers many times a day, but they stand in full view of everyone to do it, to make sure that they are seen and admired by all. They wear long, fancy robes to make sure that everyone notices them. They make sure they sit up front at feasts and at the synagogue, so that everyone knows they are there. They tell you to address them as 'Rabbi', so they can feel that they're superior to you all."

Both murmurs of agreement and gasps of shock came from the crowd.

"Well," Jesus went on, "I tell you to call no one 'Rabbi'. You have one master, who is the Christ. You have one teacher. You have one father – our Father in Heaven – and you are all brothers and sisters. I can assure you that whoever sets themselves up as superior to others will one day find themselves the lowest of the low. Whoever does their best to serve others, will one day find themselves honoured with greatness."

Jesus shook His head sadly. "Yes, I feel sorry for the scribes and Pharisees," He cried, "for they will never see heaven themselves. Worst of all, these blind fools are leading you, the general public, astray, so they're shutting the gates of the kingdom not just against themselves but against others, too."

The crowd erupted into a clamour of outrage.

"Let me give you an example," Jesus said. "They tell you that an oath on the temple is meaningless, but an oath on the sacred temple gold is binding. This is ridiculous! For which is greater: the gold or the temple which made the gold sacred? Similarly, they tell you that to swear by the altar means nothing, yet to swear by a holy altar sacrifice is to make a solemn vow! Nonsense, again! For which is greater: the sacrifice itself or the altar which makes the sacrifice holy?"

The listening men and women looked at each other. It was hard to argue with that type of logic...

Jesus continued, "So I tell you that anyone who swears by the temple swears by it and by He whose house it is!"

Ripples of applause broke out among the stunned crowd. The temple was full, and everyone was listening intently to Jesus's words.

"Furthermore," Jesus went on, "the scribes and Pharisees tell you that the hundreds of tiny rules they follow are vitally important. By doing so, they put a heavy burden on the shoulders of anyone who wants to follow God. Moreover, their preoccupation with minor matters means that they neglect the weightier matters of the law, such as justice and mercy and faith! I tell you that the scribes and Pharisees are like whitewashed tombs, which from the outside appear beautiful, but on the inside are full of dead men's bones. They are the sons of those men who, through history, were so blinded by their own self-righteousness that they refused to listen to the prophets. Even today, they are persecuting, driving out and killing the very people sent by God to help and warn them. O Jerusalem! How many times have I tried to show you the way to salvation? Yet your house is tumbling into ruins! You will not see me again until you say, 'Blessed is He who comes in the name of the Lord.'"

Jesus looked around at the hundreds of faces in the crowd. Angry discussions were breaking out between those who agreed with His criticism of the elders and those who thought He had gone too far. Jesus could see that many of the men and women hadn't really grasped what He meant.

His eyes fell on a tiny, bent-over old woman, hobbling to the temple collection box on crooked legs. Younger, richer people were sweeping past her, nearly knocking her over. One by one, they dropped in their handful of silver or gold with a smile of self-satisfaction and stalked away, head held high. Eventually, the poor widow reached the collection box for her turn. She shoved a shaky hand into her tattered pocket and brought out two coppers – the only money she had left in all the world. She dropped the coins into the box without a moment's hesitation and stood for a while, saying a silent prayer, before hobbling away.

Jesus smiled, and pointed the poor and feeble woman out to everyone in the crowd that had gathered around Him.

> ❝ *Truly, I tell you, this poor widow has put in more than all of them.* ❞

"That widow has done more good than all the scribes and Pharisees put together," He told the hushed throng. "For they only donate as much as they reckon they can afford, making sure they still have riches left over. This woman has very little, yet she has given it all for the love of God."

Synagogues
A synagogue is the Jewish place of worship. It also serves as a centre for the Jewish community. There are religious services three times a day, with readings and prayers. The religious teacher at the synagogue is called the rabbi. Synagogues may date back to the exile in Babylon in the 500s BC, when the people were far from Jerusalem and had no temple. By the time of Jesus, most Jews outside Jerusalem came together on the sabbath at their local synagogue.

❧ ABOUT THE STORY ❧
Many people think that pleasing God is a matter of keeping certain rules. That is quite natural. Rules give us a structure for daily life. Jesus never said we should ignore God's rules; He encouraged people to keep them. The rules the Pharisees kept had been made up by them. They were customs. The main rules that God and Jesus want us to keep are to love God from our hearts, and to love others as we do ourselves.

The End of the World

JESUS headed back to Bethany for the night. His footsteps were heavy as He trudged wearily along the road, His mind full of the troubles that He knew were close at hand. Jesus began to silently pray to His Father in heaven, asking for guidance and courage. Suddenly His thoughts were disturbed by gasps of awe from His disciples behind Him.

"Look, Master!" came their voices. "How wonderful!"

Jesus spun round to see what His disciples were marvelling at – a fantastic view of the whole of Jerusalem, glowing in the setting sun. The huddles of whitewashed houses nestling in the hills were shimmering pink and orange. The gardens that overflowed down the slopes were flooded with rosy light. Towering over everything, the holy temple itself was ablaze against the skyline, golden fire rippling across its pillars.

"The house of God is truly magnificent!" the disciples cried. "Absolutely breathtaking!"

Jesus nodded His head sadly.

"Take a good look," He said, "and remember. For I tell you that the day will come when not a single stone of all this will remain standing."

With that, Jesus turned back on His way, leaving His disciples puzzled, murmuring among themselves.

"Whatever can He mean?" they wondered, hurrying to catch up. "How would the temple be destroyed? When? Who would dare to pull it down?"

Later, Peter, James, John and Andrew drew Jesus to one side and spoke with Him in private.

"Lord, can you tell us when the end will be?" they asked Jesus. "What signs will there be to show us that it's about to happen?"

Jesus sat quietly for a while, His all-seeing eyes gazing far off into the distance. Then He looked at His friends and sighed.

"The end will not come," He said, "until nation has risen against nation, and kingdom against kingdom. There will be wars and earthquakes and famines, and this will still only be the beginning. Before the time draws near, my gospel must be preached throughout the world to all peoples. You who follow me and who spread my teachings will be persecuted for my sake – even by those whom you most love. You will suffer being beaten and put on trial and even executed. You must have courage to be my witness in spite of it all. The Holy Spirit will tell you what to

say and will give you the strength to endure through everything that is sent to test you. In the end, whoever has stood firm will be saved.

"Be very careful that no one leads you astray. There will be many who come in my name, saying, 'I am the Christ', but you must not listen to these false prophets. They will

work wonders and show you great signs and warn you that the end is about to come – all to get you to abandon me and follow them. Do not believe them. Remember that I told you all this would happen, and take heart.

"When the end of time finally draws near, the sun will darken and the moon will no longer give out light. The stars will fall from the skies and the seas will rise up against the earth. People everywhere will tremble with fear and faint with terror at what is happening, for the very powers of the heavens will be shaken. But my faithful followers should not be afraid. It is then that you should raise your heads and look up with glad hearts. For your salvation will then arrive. The Son of Man will come riding on the clouds in all His glory with all the angels. He will send them out on the winds to all four corners of the earth, and He will gather every single good person to Him.

> **" Take heed, watch; for you do not know when the time will come. "**

"When exactly this will happen, I cannot tell you. No one knows – not the angels in heaven, not the Son of Man – only the Father Himself. Be ever watchful. You do not want God to come suddenly and find you sleeping. For if the Lord comes on a day you do not expect, and you have left it too late to prepare yourself, there will be no hope for you. You will be cast out into hell, where souls suffer eternal punishment, and you will be left to weep and wail for ever in the darkness of utter despair."

❖ ABOUT THE STORY ❖

Jesus taught a lot about the future, but He never gave people enough detail to enable them to work out exactly what would happen when. In fact, "the end time" in the Bible is really the whole period between Jesus's resurrection and His return or "second coming". He says people are not to waste time trying to work out what the future will be, but to use their time wisely so that they are ready for anything.

Destroying the temple
As Jesus predicted, the temple in Jerusalem was destroyed by the Romans in AD 70. This stone relief shows them plundering the temple and stealing its treasures.

The end of the world
This is the explosion of a nuclear bomb. In the story, Jesus warns His disciples that the world will come to an end, and tells them to be prepared for this. Today, many people see the image of a nuclear explosion as a symbol of the end of the world brought about by humankind.

Judas Plots Betrayal

THE chief priests and scribes, Pharisees and Sadducees, were at their wits' end. They had tried to trick Jesus and it hadn't worked. The crafty Nazarene troublemaker had foiled every trap they had laid. No, cunning was no good. The Jewish elders would have to go back to their first option – force. They still had the same old problem – Jesus's crowds of supporters felt so passionately about their teacher that they'd fight tooth and nail to defend Him. Even though the authorities desperately wanted Jesus out of the way, they didn't want to risk their own lives in doing it.

Secretly, the Jewish elders gathered together in the palace of the high priest, Caiaphas. They brainstormed and schemed and argued long into the night, and came up with just one possibility. Sooner or later, they decided, Jesus would be on His own, without the support of His disciples. They would have to seize the moment with both hands. They would approach Jesus by surprise, backed up with troops, and arrest Him swiftly and without any fuss. The elders were determined that nothing would go wrong this time. The opportunity would be rare and they might only get one chance.

One big hurdle still remained. Even with their spies in the crowds, the Jewish dignitaries couldn't watch Jesus every minute of every day and night. After all, He was closely flanked by His 12 disciples at all times and they disappeared off together now and again in private. However were the elders going to be able to find out where and when to make their move?

Who knows, the Jewish authorities might never have got the chance at all if it hadn't been for a traitor inside the camp. Months before, Jesus had warned the disciples that one of them would turn to evil. The shocked men hadn't been able to believe it and had instantly laughed it off. Even so, the thought had haunted them for a while. Which one of them was Jesus talking about? What kind of evil could they possibly turn to? As time had passed, each one of the twelve had pushed the ridiculous thought further and further to the back of their minds until they had all totally forgotten it.

Roman atrium
Wealthy Romans such as Caiaphas would have received guests in a large hall, called an atrium, inside the front door. This picture of an atrium in Pompeii shows that the roof was open to the sky, to let in light. An atrium often contained a pool, which helped to keep it cool, as well as plants and statues.

Caiaphas's house
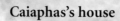
This picture shows the stone steps that lead up to Caiaphas's house. Caiaphas was the Jewish high priest and, as such, was the head of the Sanhedrin (the Jewish high court). Meetings such as the one described in this story may have been held in Caiaphas's house in order to keep them secret.

Yet Satan hadn't forgotten. He had been niggling away at the heart of Judas Iscariot for some time now, playing on his weaknesses, eating away at his doubts, filling him up with the poison of jealousy. On the fateful night that the elders sat plotting in Caiaphas's palace, Judas found that a wicked idea popped into his head as if from nowhere.

> *Then Satan entered into Judas called Iscariot, who was of the number of the twelve.*

The chief priests and scribes, Pharisees and Sadducees, never found out what made Judas Iscariot do what he did. In any case, they didn't care. In the end, they were just glad that he came knocking on their door, although at first they glowered at him with suspicion.

"Everyone knows that you're after Jesus of Nazareth," Judas swaggered. "Well, I'm one of His most trusted friends."

"Y-e-s," the high priest uttered in a low voice. "Go on..."

Under Caiaphas's stony gaze, beads of sweat began to break out on Judas's forehead. His dull eyes blinked shiftily.

"Surely I'm exactly what you need. Someone who can get closer to Jesus than you ever could," he blustered, "if the price is right, of course."

An excited murmur went round the table and eager smiles lit up the elders' wrinkled faces. They could hardly believe their good fortune! Urgently, the corrupt officials huddled together and discussed for a while.

It seemed like a lifetime to Judas, all alone in the middle of Caiaphas's great hall, with his heart pounding inside his chest. Finally, the Jewish elders settled themselves back into their chairs and arranged their robes around them.

"We will pay you thirty pieces of silver for delivering Jesus of Nazareth into our hands," they announced haughtily. "No more and no less."

Judas swallowed hard.

"Done," he said.

After a quick drink with his new friends to seal the matter, he hurried off into the night. There wasn't a moment to lose if he was going to claim that reward.

Love of money
The Jewish priests hand over the money to Judas. Judas is prepared to betray Jesus to satisfy his own greed. The Bible states that you cannot serve both God and money, and that money should be valued for what can be done with it, not in its own right.

❧ ABOUT THE STORY ❧

No one knows exactly why Judas betrayed Jesus. He seems to have been a loyal member of the disciples up until now. He was probably motivated by several reasons, money being the least of them. He may have been very mixed up about who Jesus was and what He had come to do. Maybe he thought this action would help. His action, though, warns readers that even those closest to Jesus can turn from Him, or even against Him.

Jesus Faces His Betrayer

Jesus knew that time was running out. He would very soon be leaving the troubles and wickedness of this world and would return to His Father in heaven. He was filled with great sadness at the thought of leaving behind all those He loved on earth. He and His 12 closest friends would be able to share just one more evening together – the Passover supper. Yet in order to enjoy each other's company for the last time, the arrangements had to be highly secret, so Jesus's enemies couldn't find Him.

"Go into Jerusalem and watch for a man carrying a pitcher of water to pass by," Jesus instructed two of His disciples. "Follow him and he will lead you to a certain house. Ask the owner of the house to show you where your teacher is to celebrate the Passover. You will then be taken to a large upstairs room where you'll find all you need to make everything ready."

Later that evening, the disciples made their way cautiously to the appointed meeting place. Their mood was serious. It certainly wasn't going to be the joyful Passover supper of previous years. This time, everyone was deeply worried. Only two days before, Jesus had warned His friends once again that He was soon to fall into the hands of His opponents and that they would put Him to death. Even though the disciples still couldn't

bring themselves to believe it, they were all very on edge. It was an extremely sombre group of men who sat down to eat that night.

The disciples were stirred from their grim thoughts when Jesus suddenly stood up, took off His outer robes, tied a towel around His waist and filled a bowl with water. They realized with shock that He was preparing Himself to wash the dust from their feet – a job usually done by the lowliest servants.

When Jesus came and knelt down beside Peter, who was horrified.

"Master, I can't allow you to do that for me!" Peter cried, laying hold of Jesus's hands.

"You don't understand now what I'm doing," Jesus replied, "but trust me – later you will." Peter was adamant and swung his legs out of reach.

"I'll never let you wash my feet, Lord," he said, firmly.

"Then I can't call you my friend," Jesus said to him with a sad smile.

"Well, in that case, wash my head and hands too!" Peter urged his friend and master.

"No," said Jesus, gently wetting Peter's feet. "Anyone who bathes needs only to have their feet washed to take away the dust from the road."

Jesus busied Himself with the towel.

"All of you are clean – except for one," He said to

Jesus the servant
Jesus took on the role of a servant and washed His disciples' feet. He taught His followers to serve each other as equals.

Footwashing
Most people wore open sandals, so their feet quickly became dirty. It was therefore customary for guests to have their feet washed on arrival at a house. A servant would usually carry out this task, using a water bowl like the one shown here.

Himself. He moved around the group of friends, attending to them in turn, and returned to His place at the table.

"You call me 'teacher' and 'Lord'," He said to the 12 companions, "and that's what I am. Just as I have stooped to wash your feet, so you should humble yourselves before others. Remember that a servant is not greater than his master, and always show other people the kindness, care and respect that I have shown you today."

Jesus paused for a moment and sighed a heavy sigh. His brow grew furrowed and His face darkened.

> ## *For He knew who was to betray Him.*

"One of you will betray me," He said in a low voice.

Hurt cries of protest went up from all around the table, and Jesus held up His hand for quiet. He refused to say anything more and motioned for everyone to return to their meal.

As the disciples went back to their eating and chatting, Peter found he had suddenly lost his appetite. He signalled to John, who was sitting nearest to Jesus.

"Please ask Jesus to tell us who He means," Peter whispered.

John leant over for a moment and murmured to His master, and the hushed answer came back, "The one to whom I will give this bread."

Peter watched as, slowly and deliberately, Jesus tore off a piece of His bread, dipped it into the dish in front of Him and offered it to Judas Iscariot.

"Do what you have to do," Jesus said quietly, "but do it quickly."

Without a word, Judas got up from the table and left the room.

The disciples who noticed him go thought that Jesus was sending him on some sort of errand – perhaps to buy some more wine, or to go to distribute some food to the poor. They didn't give him more than a sideways glance.

Yet Jesus had looked deep into Judas's eyes. He had seen that they were cold and hard.

Teachers and pupils

Much of Jesus's teaching took place in the temple, which was officially used as a school for Jewish children. Many Roman children, though, did not go to school as they had to work. Richer children went to a primary school between the ages of six and eleven. After this, some boys went to a secondary school.

The Last Supper

JESUS motioned for His 11 friends around the table to fall quiet. Soon, all attention was fixed firmly on Him.

Jesus reached out for a hunk of bread. He shut His eyes and lifted the bread up heavenwards. Loud and clear, He said a blessing over it, giving thanks to God. Then Jesus broke the bread into pieces and handed it round to each of the disciples.

"Take it... eat it..." He said, pressing the bits of bread into His friends' hands. "This is my body, which will be given up for you."

The wide-eyed men did as their master instructed.

Next, Jesus poured some wine. He reverently lifted the goblet up and blessed it, praising aloud to God. Then Jesus held the brimming cup out to His friends. "Take this, all of you, and drink from it," He said. "This is my blood, the seal of a new and everlasting promise from God. My blood will be spilt for you and for all people so that your sins may be forgiven."

> " *This is my body which is given for you. Do this in remembrance of me.* "

One by one, the disciples took the goblet to their lips and drank.

"I am giving you a new commandment," Jesus told them. "To love each other as I have loved you. Then everyone will know that you are my followers. May my peace always be with you. Don't let your hearts be troubled, and don't be afraid. Just follow everything that I have told you and be joyful. For you will know that I am alive in the Father, that you are alive in me, and that I am alive in you. If you keep my commandments, you will show that you truly love me. My Father in turn will love you."

Jesus rose to His feet. "Now come," He said, opening His arms and smiling at His friends. "Accompany me to the Mount of Olives. I should like to pray for a while in the Garden of Gethsemane."

As they walked through the moonlight, Jesus continued to talk. He had many things still to tell the disciples and only a little time left in which to say them.

"I want you to do the things I've done tonight as a way of remembering me," Jesus told the disciples. "For I will be with you only a short while longer and then I must go away. Where I am going, you cannot follow."

The disciples turned to each other in disbelief.

"Lord, where are you going?" Peter cried.

"I will not leave you for ever," Jesus consoled. "I am going to prepare a place for you in my Father's house. I will return a while, and then I will have to go away again. Even though you won't be able to see me anymore, I'll always be with you – inside your hearts. Later on, when the time comes, you will follow me and we will all be together again."

Peter couldn't bear the thought of Jesus leaving them. "No!" he insisted, stopping in his tracks. "Why can't we follow you now?"

Jesus looked at His companions sadly. "By the end of the night, you will all have deserted me," He said.

Site of the supper
Jesus's last meal with His disciples is traditionally believed to have been held in the building shown above. It is called the Coenaculum and is situated on Mount Zion in Jerusalem.

The Holy Grail
In medieval legend, the Holy Grail is the cup used by Jesus at the Last Supper, or the dish that was on the table during the meal. The medieval knights of the Round Table went on quests to find the Grail, which are described in the stories of King Arthur, written from the 1200s onwards. The word "grail" comes from the Old French word "greal", meaning a kind of dish. The image of the Grail is also used to represent the human body containing the Holy Spirit.

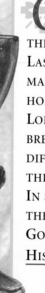

CHRISTIANS HAVE DIFFERENT VIEWS ABOUT THE WAY THEY SHOULD CELEBRATE THIS LAST SUPPER. SOME CALL IT MASS, OTHERS EUCHARIST OR HOLY COMMUNION, SOME THE LORD'S SUPPER OR BREAKING OF BREAD. FOR ALL THEIR DIFFERENCES, THEY AGREE THAT THIS IS THE CENTRE OF WORSHIP. IN SHARING BREAD AND WINE, THEY SHOW THEY DEPEND ON GOD AND WANT TO DRAW ON HIS GRACE FOR THEIR LIVES. ❧

"Not me!" Peter cried. "I will never desert you! I would lay down my life for you!"

There was a chorus of agreement from the other disciples, who were just as shocked.

"Would you, Peter?" Jesus said softly. "My friend, before you hear the cock crow to greet the dawn, you will have denied three times that you know me."

Peter almost wept.

"I will never deny that I know you," he gulped, "even if it means that I have to die with you."

❧ ABOUT THE STORY ❧

The Last Supper took place during a Jewish Passover meal. During the meal, there were a number of symbolic actions which reminded people of what God had done for them. Among these actions were the sharing of bread and wine. Jesus took these and gave them a new meaning. God was making a new agreement with His people, sealed by the death of Jesus and setting them free from slavery to sin and death.

Remembering Jesus
This is a picture of the Last Supper by the Italian artist Leonardo Da Vinci. Christians today commemorate Jesus's last meal with His disciples by eating and drinking holy bread and wine. The bread and wine are referred to as the body and the blood of Christ.

In the Garden of Gethsemane

IN the Garden of Gethsemane, the disciples yawned wearily. "Stay here and rest," Jesus said kindly to the disciples.

As the grateful men began to collapse to the ground, Jesus stopped Peter, James and John.

"My friends, I know you are tired too," He said, "but would you keep me company?"

The three disciples saw that Jesus's face was creased with sorrow and His eyes sparkled oddly. They accompanied Him further on. They had never seen Jesus so sad and troubled before. "I must be on my own to talk to my Father," He said. "My heart is so heavy, I fear it is breaking. Will you watch over me while I pray?"

Peter, James and John looked on helplessly as Jesus sank to His knees, clutching His head in His hands.

"Oh my Father!" Jesus cried out from His soul.

He felt the sins of all the world pressing in on Him from all sides, and He knew the horror of what lay ahead. "Father, nothing is impossible for you. I beg you, please take away the suffering that I have to face."

Jesus prayed for a long while and Peter, James and John were overcome by sleep. "Couldn't you have stayed awake just one more hour for me?" Jesus whispered to them. "Be careful of temptation," He said, softly. "Your spirits are willing, but your flesh is weak."

Again He prayed, "If this torment must come, then I will endure it. Your will, not mine, should be done."

Eventually Jesus arose and went back to His friends.

"I beg you, wake up!" He whispered urgently.

The three exhausted men stirred, but didn't wake.

Trembling, Jesus returned to His lonely prayers.

"Father, I know the hour has come," He groaned. "Give me the strength to die gloriously. Holy Father, look after these people so they may reach you safely. I pray also for those whom I haven't met, but who believe because they hear about me through others."

> ❝ *Judas, would you betray the Son of Man with a kiss?* ❞

Jesus returned one last time to Peter, James and John.

"Are you still sleeping?" He murmured. "No matter. It's time. Look, my betrayer is here."

Suddenly, flaming torches came flashing through the dark. Shadows loomed forwards from all around.

The disciples woke and dashed to Jesus's side. They faced a band of armed men – hired hands of the elders.

WE DON'T OFTEN THINK OF JESUS NEEDING US, ONLY OF US NEEDING HIM. HOWEVER, ON THIS OCCASION, WHEN HE NEEDED HIS FRIENDS TO ENCOURAGE AND HELP HIM THEY FAILED. TODAY, JESUS NEEDS PEOPLE TO BE HIS HANDS AND HIS VOICE IN THE WORLD. EACH TIME HE IS LET DOWN, HIS TEARS FLOW AGAIN. ❧

Jesus's retreat
The Garden of Gethsemane was situated to the east of Jerusalem, near the Mount of Olives. In Hebrew, "Gethsemane" means "oil press", and this is where the mountain olives were brought to be pressed into oil.

Kneeling to pray
Jesus and his disciples often went to pray in the Garden of Gethsemane. The way Jesus went down on his knees to pray gave rise to the Christian custom of kneeling to pray.

"Who are you looking for?" Jesus asked.

"Jesus of Nazareth!" the men shouted angrily.

"I am He," announced Jesus.

There was something so powerful in His voice and manner that the thugs shrank back nervously.

Then a face the disciples knew well came forward.

"Master!" said Judas Iscariot, greeting Jesus with his usual embrace.

"Oh Judas," Jesus sighed sadly, "must you betray me with a kiss?"

It was the sign the thugs had been waiting for and they leapt forwards to seize their enemy.

Jesus didn't resist, but the disciples flung themselves at the soldiers. Peter had brought a sword, but his wild slashes only cut off the right ear of the high priest's servant.

"Enough!" roared Jesus. "Put away your sword, Peter, for those who use violence die by violence. If my Father meant for me to be protected, armies of angels would speed to my rescue."

Jesus touched the wound. At once, the ear was healed.

Then Jesus turned to the mob.

"Am I a criminal, that you come to take me like this?" He demanded. "Every day I was there in the temple. Yet this fulfils the prophecies. It is evil's greatest hour."

With that, Jesus was marched away. Panic broke out among his followers, and as the remaining guards turned on the yelling crowd, the disciples fled for their lives.

Betrayed with a kiss
When Judas kisses Jesus, he is giving a signal to the soldiers. Jesus is sad that His disciple has betrayed Him with a kiss, which was normally given as a sign of affection or respect.

Christ's passion
Jesus expressed His anguish at His fate in a prayer to God. He knew that His mental pain would be even worse than the physical punishment He was to endure.

❖ ABOUT THE STORY ❖

Jesus knew, and He had always known, that He would be crucified in Jerusalem. He had foretold it often enough to his apostles, but knowing it did not make it any easier. Crucifixion was a horrible, painful way to die. The human side of Jesus almost opted out of His divine calling. Despite His struggle with His natural human fears, He knew that God's eternal will was more important than His short-term suffering.

Peter's Denial

MARCHING along to the soldiers' rhythm, Jesus saw the mighty city of Jerusalem rearing up in front of Him. Guards held Him tight on either side and lowered spears were aimed at the ready at His back. Without slowing the pace, the soldiers tramped straight through the city gates and along the streets to the grand house of Caiaphas, the high priest. All the time, following behind them was Peter, cloaked by the night. He made sure he kept at a safe distance, but he didn't let Jesus out of his sight for a single instant. Peter even followed the soldiers right into Caiaphas's courtyard. Then he could go no further. Jesus was taken through Caiaphas's huge front doors and they slammed shut. Peter's friend had disappeared from view and he himself was shut out in the cold.

Peter turned and found himself looking into the curious faces of strangers. The high priest's servants and maids had built themselves a fire in the middle of the courtyard, and they were huddled around it to keep warm. Trying not to draw any more attention to himself, Peter drew his robe further over his face and lowered his head. He edged nearer the circle of people to join them and did his best to enter into the general conversation.

Even though Peter was now standing near to the blazing fire, nothing could take away the cold fear that grasped his heart. Ice seemed to be running through his veins and it was as if an empty blackness was eating away at his stomach. Peter shuddered, and a serving maid peered at him through the flickering flames. A look of recognition crossed her face and she pointed her finger at him.

"You're one of the prisoner's followers, aren't you?" she blurted out.

Peter's heart began to race. Here he was, all alone in the midst of his enemies.

"Of course not!" he muttered. "I don't know what you mean."

Very gradually, Peter shifted into the shadows a little.

As he sat alone and shivered, footsteps drew near.

"You are," said another serving maid, looking hard into Peter's face.

She raised her voice to her colleagues around the fire. "This man was with Jesus of Nazareth," she cried.

"No I wasn't," Peter insisted frantically. "I don't know anyone of that name."

He gathered his robes more tightly round him and hoped desperately that no one would notice he was breaking out into a cold sweat.

"You must be one of Jesus's followers," said a servant, coming right up close. "You speak with a Galilean accent."

The crowing of the cock
Many people kept poultry, and the sound of a cock crowing at dawn would have been a familiar one. It was a signal that the night was over and the next day was beginning.

Peter
When Peter denies knowing Jesus it is an example of human weakness. Even the most dedicated followers of Jesus are vulnerable when their loyalty is tested. This reminds us that only God can provide us with the strength to avoid temptation.

Galilee
The area in northern Israel where Jesus and Peter grew up is called Galilee. It is mostly hilly, with a large lake known as the Sea of Galilee. Galilee was a much wealthier region than Judea, having made the most of the Roman occupation, and its people were not popular in Jerusalem. The people who accused Peter recognised his strong Galilean accent.

"Yes," said another, moving in towards them. "Didn't I see you in the garden with Him?"

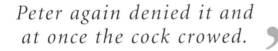

> *Peter again denied it and at once the cock crowed.*

Peter sprang to his feet in terror. His voice was high and shrill. "I've told you!" he cried. "I don't know the man!"

As the servants nervously backed away, a raucous noise ripped through the air – the sound of a cockerel. Peter's heart began to pound in his chest as he remembered Jesus's words: "My friend, before you hear the cock crow to greet the dawn, you will have denied three times that you know me." Then the tears began to pour uncontrollably from Peter's eyes and, filled with utter misery and sadness, he stole away to be on his own with his shame.

Peter's weakness

Peter denies that he knows Jesus. When Jesus had predicted this, Peter had been adamant that he would die before denying Him. However, concern for his own safety took precedence and Peter was not strong enough to stand by his master and friend. Jesus had known this would happen.

Armed with spears

The soldiers who arrested Jesus would have carried spears similar to the ones shown here. Earlier spears had now been replaced by the heavy javelin (called a *pilum*), which had a sharp, narrow point. The javelin was thrown through the air and its point could pierce the shield and even the armour of an enemy.

❖ ABOUT THE STORY ❖

While he was with Jesus and the other disciples, Peter was brave and determined. Once he was on his own, his courage melted away. He was confused and frightened. This story shows the human side of one of Jesus's greatest followers. It shows that even the best can fail, even when they expect to succeed. Peter's mistake was to stop trusting God just when he needed to trust Him. The good news was that later, Peter was forgiven.

Trial Before the Sanhedrin

CAIAPHAS'S palace was filled with a sinister silence. Jesus's footsteps echoed as he was marched down the long corridors, then through a big, heavy door. Jesus found himself in an important looking chamber. Annas, the former high priest, was standing at the window. "So this is the famous Jesus of Nazareth," he said.

He looked Jesus straight in the eye.

"I've heard so much about you," he said, with a stony smile, "but I'd rather hear it from your own lips."

Then the questioning started. What did Jesus think about the scriptures? What miracles did He claim to have worked? Who did He think He was? Throughout it all, Jesus remained quiet and calm. He didn't say a word, even when Annas peered closely into His face. Finally, the former high priest lost his temper.

"Answer me!" he spat. "Or I'll have you thrown into prison until you find your tongue!"

"I have always spoken openly," Jesus replied softly. "I have preached in public. I have never taught in secret, so why ask me about my work? Why don't you ask any of the people who came to hear me?"

SMACK! A guard's hand stung Jesus's cheek. "Is that how you talk to your betters?" the soldier raged.

"If I have said anything wrong, explain to me what it is," Jesus said. "If not, why have you hit me?"

Annas had had enough. He was getting nowhere.

"Take him away!" he barked.

Jesus was marched off to Caiaphas, the high priest, and the council of Jewish elders, the Sanhedrin. The officials

Money changers
The priests in the story are described as corrupt because they took advantage of their positions to increase their own wealth. They insisted that only one currency was used to pay taxes at the temple and to buy sacrificial animals. Money changers exchanged currency for the worshippers at the temple, charging them for this service. The priests claimed part of the proceeds for themselves, and this was one of the things for which Jesus condemned them.

Public meetings
Jesus used to preach a great deal in public places. He often used open spaces in the countryside so all the people could hear Him. The Romans built these buildings called amphitheatres specifically for large meetings, and to hold plays and games.

began to fire false accusations at Jesus. They even brought out false witnesses whom they'd bribed with money. Yet no two witnesses could be found to agree on a story.

Eventually, a couple of men came forward.

"We both heard this man say that He could destroy the temple of God and rebuild it in three days," they agreed.

Jesus had said this, but He had been referring to His own body. He was foretelling that He would be raised up to life three days after His death. The men, like most people, had misunderstood.

> ## "I have said nothing secretly"

"Have you nothing to say to that?" Caiaphas raged. Still Jesus didn't move a muscle.

"Right!" Caiaphas yelled, losing all patience. "I order you to tell us, under solemn oath, whether you think you're the Son of God!"

When Jesus spoke, there was majesty in His voice.

"I am," he said, "and one day you will see the Son of Man seated at the right hand of the Father in Heaven."

"Blasphemy!" Caiaphas bellowed, purple with fury. "He has insulted God! What shall we do with Him?"

"Put Him to death!" the elders roared.

At long last, they had Jesus where they wanted. They blindfolded Him and spat on Him, and punched and kicked Him, saying, "Let's hear you prophesy, now, Christ! Tell us who it was that struck you!" Their laughter rang through the night.

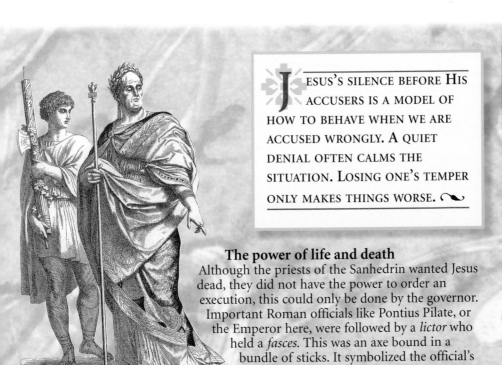

JESUS'S SILENCE BEFORE HIS ACCUSERS IS A MODEL OF HOW TO BEHAVE WHEN WE ARE ACCUSED WRONGLY. A QUIET DENIAL OFTEN CALMS THE SITUATION. LOSING ONE'S TEMPER ONLY MAKES THINGS WORSE.

The power of life and death
Although the priests of the Sanhedrin wanted Jesus dead, they did not have the power to order an execution, this could only be done by the governor. Important Roman officials like Pontius Pilate, or the Emperor here, were followed by a *lictor* who held a *fasces*. This was an axe bound in a bundle of sticks. It symbolized the official's power to punish and execute people.

❖ ABOUT THE STORY ❖

When Jesus first mentioned to His apostles that He was the Son of God, He made it clear to them that they were not to tell anyone. He did this because people were expecting the Messiah to be an earthly soldier and leader who would fight the Romans and force them to leave Judea. However, now Jesus knows that the time for Him to reveal the truth has arrived. He can tell the truth, and the prophecies will be fulfilled by Him.

Pontius Pilate

Even though the chief priests and scribes had passed sentence, one more hurdle lay in front of them: an execution could only be ordered by the Roman governor, Pontius Pilate. They didn't have a moment to waste...

The whole of Jerusalem awoke that morning to the news that the elders had condemned Jesus of Nazareth to death. When the gossip reached the ears of Judas Iscariot, he was totally appalled at what he had done. Filled with shame and remorse, he tore to the temple as fast as he could to try to put things right.

"I have committed a terrible sin!" he cried to the chief priests. "Jesus is innocent and I have betrayed Him!"

The Jewish officials just stared at Judas coldly. "That's not our problem," they said. "It's yours."

Despair flooded over Judas. He threw his thirty pieces of silver onto the temple floor and ran out into the city streets. Later, Judas Iscariot's body was found hanging. He was too disgusted with himself to go on living.

Meanwhile, in another part of the city, Jesus was standing in Pontius Pilate's judgement hall. The Roman governor looked at the weary, bruised man and then said, "So, are you the King of the Jews?"

"Are you asking me this for yourself," Jesus replied softly to the governor, "or because you've heard other people say it about me?"

Pilate looked away from Jesus's steady gaze. "Look," he said seriously, "your own people and priests have handed you over to me. Tell me what you've done."

"My kingship is not of this world," Jesus said. "If it were, my servants would have fought to prevent me being handed over to the Jews."

"So you are a king?" the intrigued Pilate challenged.

"Yes," said Jesus. "I was born for this and I came into the world to bear witness to the truth."

Pilate paused for a while, deep in thought.

"The Jewish elders tell me that you've been plotting against the Roman government," he said.

Jesus said nothing.

"They say that you're rousing up the Jews against us," Pilate continued, "that you're encouraging them not to pay Caesar's taxes, and setting yourself up as their leader."

Again, Jesus remained silent.

Roman Robur
When Jesus was beaten by the Roman soldiers, He was probably taken to a robur like this one. It was a pit, deep underground, for beating prisoners.

Pilate's judgement
This picture shows Jesus standing in front of the Roman governor, Pontius Pilate. Only Pilate had the authority to sentence him to death. Under Roman law, blasphemy was not a crime. So, in order to persuade Pilate to pass the death penalty, the Sanhedrin told him that Jesus was guilty of treason against Rome.

"Hmmmm," said Pilate, scratching his beard. He strode out, leaving Jesus with the guards.

"I find that this man has done nothing wrong," Pilate announced to the elders.

> **For he knew that it was out of envy that they had delivered him up.**

"He's a troublemaker!" they insisted. "He's been stirring up people all the way from His home in Galilee to Judea!"

"Galilee!" Pilate suddenly spotted a way out of this situation. "Well, if He's from Galilee, then it's Herod who should deal with Him."

Herod happened to be in Jerusalem that week, so Pilate hurriedly had Jesus marched over to see him. Jesus was soon back in Pilate's palace, though. Herod was unable to find Jesus guilty of any crime either. On top of everything, Pilate's wife said, "Last night, I had a dream about Jesus of Nazareth. He is innocent of everything that the Jews have accused Him of. Have nothing to do with Him."

That settles it, Pilate thought. The Jewish elders have delivered this man up out of envy. He strode out and found that a huge crowd had gathered outside.

"This man has done nothing to deserve death," Pilate announced to the Jewish elders and the people. "I shall have Him flogged and let Him go!"

With that, Pilate's guards dragged Jesus away to be soundly whipped.

The praetorium
The military headquarters and palace where the Roman provincial governor, such as Pontius Pilate, lived was called the praetorium. It had a large tower at each corner, as in the picture. Two of these towers overlooked the main temple. Pilate's soldiers brought Jesus to the palace's private judgment hall, where he was tried.

⬧ ABOUT THE STORY ⬧
The Sanhedrin have to send Jesus for trial to the Roman governor, as they do not have the power to order His execution themselves. However, they realise that Pilate will not listen to their complaints about Jesus's religious claims, so they tell Pilate that Jesus has been plotting against the Roman government, thinking he will be more likely to convict Jesus. The governor realises that the charges are unfounded, and releases Him.

Condemned to Die

THE Jewish authorities had done their work well. They had mingled with the crowds, persuading them that Jesus was a blasphemer and a liar. As Pilate turned to walk away into his judgement hall, the citizens of Jerusalem cried out in protest. "No!" the hundreds of men and women cried out to Pilate. "Kill him! Kill Jesus of Nazareth!"

Pilate was totally taken aback.

"Why?" he said. "Whatever has he done?"

The Roman governor felt sure that Jesus was innocent. All at once, he had an idea that would help him get Jesus off the hook. Pilate had remembered that it was the custom at Passover to release a prisoner of the people's choice. He knew that there was a murderer in the cells by the name of Barabbas. Pilate felt sure that the people of Jerusalem would much rather

have Jesus walking among them in the streets than a bloodthirsty killer.

"Who would you rather have me release?" Pilate asked the crowds. "The King of the Jews or Barabbas?"

"Not Jesus of Nazareth!" the shouts came back. "We want Barabbas released! Give us Barabbas!"

Meanwhile, the Roman governor's soldiers were taking great delight in punishing their Jewish prisoner. They had gathered the whole battalion to come and join in the fun. Armed with cruel barbed whips, they rained down blow after blow, lashing Him with all their strength. Each soldier only stopped when he was out of breath and the sweat was dripping off his forehead, then another immediately stepped forward to take his turn. Every time Jesus was forced to His knees by the constant pain, the guards hauled Him up roughly to withstand more. Their leather thongs ate into Jesus's flesh. The blood streamed off His body and ran along the floor. Even then, the

❖ ABOUT THE STORY ❖

The charge that Jesus was the Son of God made Pilate afraid. Like many Romans, he was superstitious. He believed there were many gods, and that it was a good idea not to get on the wrong side of any of them. However, He was more concerned about getting a bad report from the Jews, which could stop him getting promotion. (Judea was not a very important posting.) So he sacrificed Jesus for himself.

Punishment before death
Jesus is flogged by the Roman soldiers. The punishment of flogging was often used before putting someone to death.

Crown of thorns
In Roman times, a crown was a symbol of royalty and kingship, just as it is today. Crowns were usually made of gold, or other precious metals, but the Roman soldiers made a crown by weaving together the stems of a thorny plant. By putting this on Jesus's head, they were making fun of the idea of Him as a king.

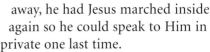

soldiers hadn't had enough. They plaited a crown of thorns, pressed it into Jesus's scalp and threw a regal purple cloak around His shoulders. The Roman guards gave Jesus a reed to hold for a royal sceptre, and propped Him up in the midst of them.

"Hail, King of the Jews!" they mocked, knocking Jesus to the floor and spitting on Him.

Suddenly, Pilate himself strode in.

"Help the man to stand and bring Him out here with me," he ordered. "Immediately!"

So Jesus was brought bleeding in His crown and cloak before the jeering crowds.

"Look!" bellowed Pilate. "Look at this man! I have not found Him guilty of anything!"

The chief priests and elders began to cry, "Crucify Him!" and the crowds quickly picked up the chant.

> " *The chief priests answered, 'We have no king but Caesar.'* "

"Take Him yourself and crucify Him!" Pilate roared, knowing that under Roman law they couldn't. "In my eyes, He's done nothing wrong!"

"By Jewish law He should die!" the Jewish officials shouted back. "He says He's the Son of God."

At that, a look of terror came over Pilate's face. Straight

away, he had Jesus marched inside again so he could speak to Him in private one last time.

"Who are you?" he urged, lifting up Jesus's drooping head. "Where have you come from?"

Jesus didn't answer.

"Why won't you speak to me?" Pilate moaned. "Don't you know that I hold in my hands the power to have you either put to death or set free?"

Jesus raised His eyes.

"You would have no power at all over me if it hadn't been given to you from above," He said quietly. Pilate made up his mind.

"I shall release this man!" he announced to the crowds.

A deafening roar of disapproval went up all around the Roman governor.

"Then you will be no friend of Caesar's," warned the chief priests. "Anyone who says they're a king is flaunting their defiance of Rome!"

The last thing Pilate wanted was to get into deep water with the emperor himself. Trembling with nerves, he called for a bowl of water and a towel. As the Roman governor washed his hands in front of everyone, the clamouring crowds fell into an expectant hush.

"I cleanse myself of this man's blood," Pilate declared.

This time, the noise that went up from the crowd was that of cheering.

Minutes later, Barabbas the murderer was released and Jesus was led out to be crucified.

Washing away the guilt
Pilate washes his hands before Jesus's crucifixion. By doing this, he was telling the crowd that he did not want to be held responsible for Jesus's death.

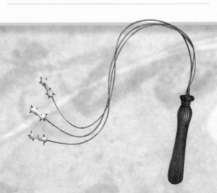

POLITICIANS TODAY VALUE PUBLIC OPINION. THEY OFTEN MAKE POLICIES TO WIN THEM VOTES. THE BIBLE REMINDS US THAT PLEASING GOD IS MORE IMPORTANT THAN PLEASING PEOPLE.

Tortured and mocked
This Roman whip is similar to the one that would have been used to flog Jesus. It consists of three leather cords attached to a handle. After Jesus had been flogged, the soldiers mocked Him by dressing Him in a purple tunic. This colour was normally worn by royalty.

Crucifixion

THE slumped figure was hardly recognizable as Jesus. The crown of thorns cut into His head. Blood ran down His battered face. His robes were stained from His wounds. Yet Jesus's kind eyes still shone with compassion. His tormentors had not broken His spirit.

The guards heaved in a solid wooden cross, twice the size of Jesus, and laid it on His back. Slowly, Jesus dragged it off through the packed streets of Jerusalem. Each step took every bit of His strength and will. Eventually, He stumbled and collapsed into the dirt, the cross crashing down on top of Him. The soldiers hauled Jesus to His feet and heaved the cross onto His back. Jesus's knees buckled and He sank to the floor, unable to move any further.

The infuriated soldiers turned towards the crowd of onlookers and dragged out a broad-shouldered man, called Simon of Cyrene. He had no choice but to carry the vicious cross on his back. Jesus staggered along behind him with two condemned thieves.

People lined the roads to see the criminals. They yelled insults and spat. Running desperately among the crowds were Jesus's friends. Many women wept bitterly, unable to turn their eyes away from Jesus's suffering, even though they could do nothing to help.

"Don't weep for me," Jesus told them, "but for yourselves and your children for the destruction which is to come."

Eventually they reached Golgotha. A soldier offered Jesus wine and pain-killing herbs, but He refused. Then came the agonising hammering – one long nail through each hand and one piercing both feet.

"Father, forgive them," cried Jesus, "for they don't know what they are doing!"

A placard was fixed above Jesus's head, reading: 'Jesus of Nazareth, King of the Jews' in three languages.

"It shouldn't say that!" the elders yelled in protest. "It should say, 'This man said, "I am King of the Jews".'"

Pontius Pilate silenced them with a glare, and they turned their attention to taunting Jesus instead.

"If you're the Son of God, come down from the cross!" the chief priests mocked.

"He said He saved others, now He can't save himself," scoffed the Pharisees.

"You said you could destroy the temple and rebuild it in three days," yelled the elders, "so why can't you get free?"

> *Father, forgive them; for they know not what they do.*

While the officials yelled their jibes, two other crosses were raised, one either side of Jesus's twisted body.

"You said you were the Christ," sneered one of the thieves. "So save yourself and us too!"

"How dare you!" gasped the other thief. "We deserve our punishment, but this man is innocent! Lord, remember me when you reach your kingdom."

"I promise you," Jesus whispered, "today you will be with me in paradise."

Suddenly darkness fell over the whole land. A cold wind screeched, drowning out the soldiers at the foot of the cross who were casting lots for Jesus's clothes.

All those who loved Jesus clung together in grief, as close to the cross as they dared. Among them were Jesus's mother Mary, the disciple John, and Jesus's friends Mary Magdalene and Salome.

"Mother," came Jesus's voice, "look after John as your son. John, take care of my mother as your own."

For three long hours, the weeping friends watched Jesus's silent agony. Then suddenly His voice rang out: "My God, my God! Why have you abandoned me?"

One of the mourners rushed to lift a stick with a sponge of wine on the end for Jesus to drink.

"Father, I give up my spirit into your hands," He cried loudly. "It is finished!" His head drooped

At that moment, a great storm broke. The ground shook and rocks split open. The veil which hung in the temple ripped into two. Some people later swore that they saw graves open and spirits rise out of them.

The Roman centurion at the foot of the cross gasped, "This man truly was the Son of God."

And terror struck the hearts of everyone at Golgotha.

Golgotha
It is not known exactly where Golgotha was, but it is often thought to be this hill outside Jerusalem.

Simon of Cyrene
The man who carried the cross for Jesus, Simon of Cyrene, was probably a pilgrim visiting Jerusalem for the Passover. Cyrene was a city in North Africa, with a large Jewish population.

❧ ABOUT THE STORY ❧

This story is packed with symbolism. Jesus refuses the wine to dull the pain, because He has to carry the weight of sin without help. Darkness falls as a sign that Jesus has been cut off from God. Pilate is more accurate with his placard than the religious leaders realized.

Jesus is Buried

THE dead body of Jesus hung on the cross until evening was drawing near. Then the Jewish elders began to grow rather agitated. Sunset would mark the start of the Sabbath, and the holy day would be made unclean if the men weren't taken down from their crosses, and the thieves that had been crucified with Jesus were still alive.

The Roman soldiers didn't need much encouraging. Glad to speed things up, they marched over to the thieves and broke their legs with a couple of savage blows. The robbers sank down under their own weight, making it impossible for them to breathe. Within minutes, they had suffocated to death.

The soldiers didn't bother doing the same to Jesus – everyone knew that He was already dead. As the Romans walked away, one soldier spitefully thrust his spear as deep as he could into Jesus's side, just for good measure. Jesus's watching friends saw blood and water gush from the wound. They shuddered and turned away in horror.

As dusk began to fall on the city of Jerusalem, Pontius Pilate sat alone, brooding on the death of Jesus of Nazareth. A servant disturbed the Roman governor from his troubled thoughts to tell him that a wealthy member of the Sanhedrin was begging to see Pilate at once.

When the visitor was ushered in, Pilate was mightily relieved to find it was Joseph of Arimathea, a Jewish official widely held to be good and just and fair.

Joseph bowed low. "Sir," he began, "I come to confess a secret. I myself am one of the followers of Jesus of

Roman burial urn
Jesus's body was buried, but some Romans at this time had their bodies cremated and the remains put into urns. This marble burial urn contains the ashes of a woman called Bovia Procula. The inscription on the urn describes her as a "most unfortunate mother". This may mean that she died during childbirth, as many women did at this time.

Jesus and Nicodemus
This bronze carving shows Jesus talking to Nicodemus, a Pharisee who came to Him for secret teaching. Not much is known about Nicodemus, but he was probably a member of the Sanhedrin.

Harrowing of Hell
This Greek Orthodox icon shows Jesus going down to Hell after His death. In medieval times, this episode was called the "Harrowing of Hell".

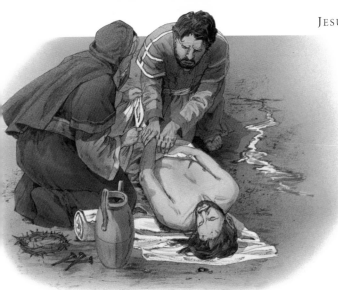

Nazareth," Joseph continued, "although I did not tell my colleagues who, as you well know, envied and hated Him. I was one of the few on the Sanhedrin who voted against this innocent man's death. Now I have come to ask a favour. Please allow me to take Jesus's body down from the cross and bury it."

> *Joseph took the body and laid it in his own new tomb.*

Pilate didn't have to think twice. "Very well," he said.

So it was that, in the dim evening light, a member of the very Council that had bayed for Jesus's blood, tenderly recovered His body from the cross. A friend called Nicodemus had brought burial spices of myrrh and aloes, and he and Joseph hurriedly wrapped Jesus in a linen shroud. Together, the two men carried Jesus's body to a nearby garden cemetery, and the women who had been friends of Jesus followed close behind, wailing aloud. A small cave-like tomb had been carved out – the tomb that

Joseph had prepared for his own burial – and they laid Jesus inside. Then Joseph and Nicodemus rolled a heavy stone in front of the tomb to close it up. There was nothing more that could be done, and at last everyone went their own sad way into the night.

Meanwhile, an extremely annoyed Pilate was busy giving an audience to yet more callers from the Sanhedrin.

"Sir, when that imposter was alive, He said He'd rise up to life again after three days," the officials said. "Therefore, order a guard to be set around the tomb until the third day, so His friends can't come and steal the body and trick everyone into thinking His words have come true."

"You have your guard!" roared Pilate.

By the time darkness had fallen, armed guards were the only living things in the garden of graves where Jesus lay.

Myrrh and aloes
In the story, Nicodemus provides expensive spices for Jesus's burial. Myrrh is a sweet-smelling gum from the bark of a tree. Aloes is the bitter juice of the aloe plant. Before burial, the body was washed and wrapped in a linen cloth, and the head was wrapped in a linen square. The spices would have been put between the folds of linen.

Joseph of Arimathea
Joseph of Arimathea carries two flasks containing Jesus's sweat and blood. With Nicodemus, Joseph prepared Jesus's body for burial

❖ ABOUT THE STORY ❖

There was no doubt that Jesus died. Roman soldiers had seen many dead bodies; they knew all the signs. The blood and water is a sign for later readers, however. It showed that the red and white cells of Jesus's blood had begun to separate around the heart, which happens after death. There was no trickery or mistake which caused Jesus to live on. Furthermore, the Gospel writers saw Jesus's death as a fulfilment of Old Testament prophecy.

Jesus Disappears

THE torches of the Sanhedrin's guard flickered outside Jesus's tomb all night of that first Good Friday. Sitting in the cemetery among the dead, the soldiers were very glad when they saw the light of Saturday finally dawning. They kept watch all that next long day, through the evening and into Saturday night. As it grew closer to the dawn of the third day after Jesus's death, the soldiers became increasingly jumpy. The Sanhedrin had assured them that they only had to fear the living, not the dead. They were on the lookout only for Jesus's friends coming to steal the body, not for ghosts. No, those haughty Jewish officials certainly didn't believe that a dead man was going to come walking out among them – but then they weren't sitting in front of the tomb, were they?

> " *Tell people, 'His disciples came by night and stole Him away while we were asleep.'* "

When the first light of the sun crept over the horizon on Sunday morning, the soldiers kept their eyes open, brandishing their spears and swords at the slightest rustle of the birds among the bushes.

Suddenly, the earth began to tremble under the soldiers' feet. It began to shake so violently that the guards were flung headlong on to the ground. A searing white light blazed out of the sky and descended over the tomb, dazzling the soldiers where they lay. They peered through their fingers and saw with astonishment that a man as luminous as lightning, as white as snow, was rolling away the massive stone from the entrance of the tomb. Nearly paralysed with fear, the cowering soldiers managed to scramble to their feet and flee for their lives.

At the same time, a group of sorrowing women were making their way to the tomb, among them Jesus's devoted friends Mary Magdalene, Mary the mother of James and John, and Salome and Joanna. They had seen how hurriedly Joseph and Nicodemus had had to prepare Jesus's body before sundown brought the Sabbath, and the kind women meant to attend to the body properly, anointing it and wrapping it with all the customary care and attention. As the grieving friends walked along through the earliest rays of the morning sun, they worried that they might not be strong enough to move away the huge stone. When they drew close to the spot, their pulses began to race. They could see that someone had already

Easter parade
Here you can see an Easter day procession in Jerusalem. Christians are gathering to re-enact Christ's walk to Golgotha with the cross.

Ossuary
In Roman times, there were two stages to a Jewish burial. First the body was wrapped, anointed and placed in a tomb. Later, when the flesh had decayed, the family gathered up the bones and put them in a stone box called an ossuary.

done it. Hearts pounding, the women raced to the tomb. Wherever were the soldiers who had been set to guard the body? Which wicked people had got there before them? What terrible things were they doing to their beloved Jesus's body, even at that very moment?

When the first couple of women reached the tomb and squeezed inside, they screamed. Jesus's body was gone, and sitting where His body should have lain, there were two shining men in radiant clothes.

"Why are you looking for the living among the dead?" came the men's voices. "Don't you remember that the Son of Man said He'd rise on the third day?"

The startled women nearly fell over each other in their hurry to get out of the tomb. Pushing their friends before them and sobbing an explanation, they ran away as fast as their legs could carry them.

Meanwhile, the terrified guards had taken their amazing story straight to the chief priests and an emergency meeting of the Sanhedrin was called. There was much shouting and arguing, thumping of tables and blaming of each other. In the end, a desperate decision was reached.

"Take this for your troubles," the elders soothed, pushing bags of coins into the sweating hands of the pale soldiers. "When people ask you what happened, tell them that you all fell asleep on duty in the night, and that Jesus's disciples crept up on you and stole the body. If Pilate himself somehow gets to hear of this mess, we'll buy his silence too. Don't worry, just say what we've told you and we'll make sure you don't get into trouble."

That was the story that was soon spread around the Jews of Jerusalem.

Mary Magdalene
When she first met Jesus, Mary Magdalene was possessed by evil spirits. When Jesus cured her of this "illness", she became a devout follower of His. It is not clear from the Bible whether her illness was physical, mental or moral, or some combination of the three.

JESUS HAD TOLD THE DISCIPLES THAT HE WOULD RISE FROM THE DEAD, BUT THEY HAD NEVER UNDERSTOOD OR BELIEVED HIM. REAL FAITH TAKES GOD AT HIS WORD, AND EXPECTS HIM TO FULFIL IT. ❧

❧ ABOUT THE STORY ❧

The Bible writers do not tell us what happened to Jesus between His death and resurrection. There is one hint in Peter's second letter which suggests Jesus told the good news of His victory over sin and death to the people who had died before and were waiting in "Hades", or Hell. The Bible writers focus instead on the supernatural elements of the resurrection. This action, they are saying, is a miracle of God.

The Women Meet Jesus

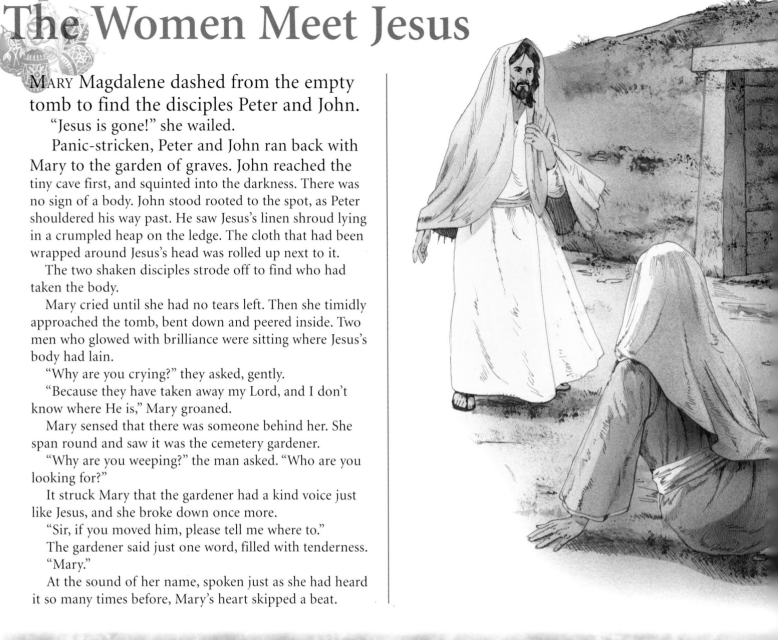

MARY Magdalene dashed from the empty tomb to find the disciples Peter and John.

"Jesus is gone!" she wailed.

Panic-stricken, Peter and John ran back with Mary to the garden of graves. John reached the tiny cave first, and squinted into the darkness. There was no sign of a body. John stood rooted to the spot, as Peter shouldered his way past. He saw Jesus's linen shroud lying in a crumpled heap on the ledge. The cloth that had been wrapped around Jesus's head was rolled up next to it.

The two shaken disciples strode off to find who had taken the body.

Mary cried until she had no tears left. Then she timidly approached the tomb, bent down and peered inside. Two men who glowed with brilliance were sitting where Jesus's body had lain.

"Why are you crying?" they asked, gently.

"Because they have taken away my Lord, and I don't know where He is," Mary groaned.

Mary sensed that there was someone behind her. She span round and saw it was the cemetery gardener.

"Why are you weeping?" the man asked. "Who are you looking for?"

It struck Mary that the gardener had a kind voice just like Jesus, and she broke down once more.

"Sir, if you moved him, please tell me where to."

The gardener said just one word, filled with tenderness. "Mary."

At the sound of her name, spoken just as she had heard it so many times before, Mary's heart skipped a beat.

The Garden Tomb
It is not known exactly where Jesus's tomb was situated. The Bible tells us only that it was in a garden near where the crucifixion took place. Christians believe its most likely location is here, a place called the Garden Tomb, in Jerusalem.

Easter eggs
In many European countries, people celebrate Easter by decorating eggs and giving them as gifts. Eggs and flowers are a symbol of new life.

"Teacher," she cried and sank to her knees, gazing up adoringly at the man she loved above all others.

"Go now," Jesus smiled. "Find my disciples and tell them that I will soon be returning to my Father."

Meanwhile, the other women who had seen the stone rolled aside were still scurrying home together in fear. All at once, they saw the dim form of a man appear in front of them in their path, and they sprang back in alarm.

"Good morning," said the figure.

The women couldn't believe their ears at the familiar voice. They fell to the ground with amazement.

"It can't be!" they whispered. "Jesus, is it really you?"

"Don't be afraid," Jesus smiled, holding His arms out towards His friends. "Go and tell my disciples to travel to Galilee, and I will meet them there soon."

> ## *Mary Magdalene went and said to the disciples, 'I have seen the Lord!'*

The vision disappeared as suddenly as it had arrived.

A little later, Mary Magdalene burst into the room where the disciples sat together in grief, red-eyed and miserable. Her face was flushed with excitement.

"I have seen the Lord !" she cried and, in a joyful tumble of words, told them everything that had happened.

The disciples shook their heads sadly. They wanted to believe Mary, but they had seen Jesus hanging on the cross with their own eyes. There was nothing anyone could say to change that.

❖ ABOUT THE STORY ❖

Many attempts have been made to "prove" that Jesus did not truly rise from the dead, and that this was a "spiritual" experience like a vision. The Gospel writers include little details that have a ring of truth. The grave clothes are lying as if the body has passed through them; Jesus did not just take them off. Grave robbers are not so careful. Mary failed to recognize Jesus because she was upset, not in a spiritual state of hope.

Jesus appears to Mary Magdalene
This painted wooden statue, dating from the 1600s, shows Mary Magdalene meeting Jesus, after He has risen from the dead. Mary Magdalene was the first person to see Jesus after the resurrection. She set off for the tomb with a group of women, but apparently ran ahead of them and arrived before them. When she discovered the tomb was empty, she immediately went to find Peter and John. After they had gone to search for the body, Mary remained alone at the tomb, weeping. It was then that she saw two angels, followed by Jesus Himself, risen from the dead.

On the Road to Emmaus

LATER on that morning of the third day, two of Jesus's disciples began walking out of Jerusalem on their way to Emmaus, a little village about eleven kilometres away. The subdued companions trudged along with heavy hearts, going over and over Jesus's sudden capture, unfair trial and terrible death. As they walked, a stranger caught up with them on the road and asked to walk with them.

"Of course, friend," replied one of the disciples, Cleopas, and then carried on with the conversation as before.

The stranger seemed puzzled.

"Can I ask what you're talking about?" He said.

Cleopas stared at the man, stunned.

"You must be the only person in the whole of Jerusalem who hasn't heard about the events of the past few days," the disciple remarked.

The stranger shrugged His shoulders innocently.

"What events?" He asked, His eyes twinkling.

"The things that have happened to Jesus of Nazareth, the greatest prophet who ever lived," replied Cleopas, reverently. "You must have heard of how our chief priests and elders seized Him, persuaded the Roman governor to condemn Him to death and then had Him crucified?"

The stranger shook His head.

"All our hope was in Jesus of Nazareth," Cleopas went on. "We had believed that He was the one sent to save us."

He paused and swallowed hard.

"Besides all of that," Cleopas continued, waving his disappointment aside, "it is now the third day since His death. Earlier on, some of the women in Jesus's company of friends brought us an amazing story about having found His tomb empty and having seen a vision of angels, who said that He was alive!"

The stranger's eyes grew wide with surprise.

"Of course," Cleopas explained, "some of us dashed straight there to see for ourselves. All we saw was that the body had indeed gone – nothing else."

The disciples hung their heads gloomily.

Suddenly the stranger seemed to know more than He

❧ ABOUT THE STORY ❧

Once again, two disciples fail to recognize Jesus. Luke brings out two important points. One is that Jesus was recognized in the breaking of bread. Christians today claim that they "meet" Jesus in a special way when they "break bread" in communion. Secondly, Jesus was known for His "burning" teaching: it gave them hope and challenged them. Today, Christians meet to hear His teaching read and explained, and to "hear" Him through it.

The resurrection

"Resurrection" means to bring a dead person back to life. "Resuscitation" can mean this too, but a resuscitated person will die eventually. Christians believe when someone is resurrected, their soul enters a new body, in which they will spend eternity.

had previously let on.

"Don't you understand what the prophets had foretold?" the man rebuked the disciples gently. "It was necessary for Christ to suffer, in order for Him to be glorified."

The stranger went on to explain the mysteries of the scriptures as the disciples had only heard Jesus explain them before. Cleopas and his companion were so fascinated by the stranger's knowledge that when they reached Emmaus and the stranger made to bid them goodbye, they begged Him not to travel on down the road but to stop with them for the evening.

So it was that the two disciples came to be having supper with the stranger. When the man took some bread and blessed it, broke it into pieces and gave it to them, the disciples at last realized who He really was.

"Jesus!" they gasped, pushing back their chairs and springing to their feet.

The stranger vanished before their very eyes.

"We should have known!" the disciples scolded each other as they hurried straight back to Jerusalem through the darkness. "Didn't your heart burn strangely within your chest as He explained everything to us?"

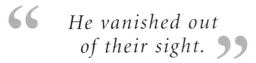

> ## He vanished out of their sight.

When the disciples reached the city, they found the disciples in a buzz of excitement. Before Cleopas and his friend could even get a word out, the disciples cried, "Peter has seen the Lord!" and dragged them into the room to tell them how Jesus had appeared to Peter and chatted with him. When the two disciples finally managed to explain how they too had met with Jesus, the room erupted in a riot of cheering and praying and weeping for joy. It seemed that Mary Magdalene's story was true, after all!

Emmaus
It is not known exactly where the village of Emmaus was situated, but some people believe it was here, at the village of Amwas, about 11km west of Jerusalem.

Jesus's last days
The Bible tells us that Jesus was resurrected on the third day. He appeared to Peter and to all the disciples, including Cleopas and his companion as they walked to Emmaus. Jesus used this time to visit His disciples, to reinforce their faith and to prove to them all that He was resurrected, that His prophecies had come true.

Doubting Thomas

JESUS's followers were jubilant, and everyone in the room wanted to talk to Peter and Cleopas and his friend at once. The disciples crowded round the three men, firing questions and praising God, begging to hear them tell again and again exactly what Jesus looked like and each word of what He said.

All at once, the hubbub died away into silence. Everyone stood stock still, staring open-mouthed at the newcomer among them. No one had heard anyone knock. No one had seen anyone enter. Yet there He was. It was Jesus.

> 66 *Jesus said to them, 'Come and have breakfast.'* 99

"Peace be with you," Jesus said, softly, greeting His friends with a familiar raise of the hand.

Everyone shrank back in fear.

"Be careful, it's a spirit!" came murmurs from the back of the room.

A frown creased Jesus's brow. "Why are you frightened?"

He asked. "I am no ghost. Look here, see the wounds on my hands and feet. It's me, Jesus."

A few of the disciples began to creep nearer, cautiously.

"Yes," urged Jesus. "Don't be afraid to touch me. See, spirits don't have flesh and bones, as you can feel that I have."

As the first trembling hands touched Jesus's warm skin, the faces of Jesus's followers brightened into delight.

"Master!" they cried. "It's really you!"

Laughing at their amazement, Jesus sat down at the table in the midst of them. Together, everyone shared a meal, just as they had done so many times before.

Now there was one disciple who wasn't present to see Jesus for himself. When Thomas later heard his friends' story – even though he saw their gladness and joy – he found the news too hard to accept.

"Unless I can touch the mark of the nails in His hands with my own fingers, and put my own hand into the wound in his side, I can't believe it," Thomas whispered.

No matter how hard he tried, he couldn't get rid of the doubts that nagged away inside him.

Eight days later, Jesus's followers were again gathered together in private, doors tightly locked against the prying

eyes of the Jewish council's spies. Just as before, halfway through the evening Jesus appeared silently among them. No one noticed His arrival.

'See my hands and my feet, that it is I myself'

"Peace be with you," He greeted his friends and turned straight to Thomas, who had shrunk back, thunderstruck.

Jesus reached out and took the terrified disciple's hands.

"Here," Jesus said, holding Thomas's fingers against the nail wounds in His palms. "Feel the wound in my side. Don't doubt any longer. Have faith. It is true."

As Thomas's fingers sank into Jesus's flesh, he broke down and wept.

"My Lord and my God!" he cried.

"You believe now because you have seen me for yourself," Jesus said, gently. "Even more blessed are those who don't see me and yet still believe."

MOST PEOPLE HAVE DOUBTS. IN FACT, IT WOULD BE TRUE TO SAY THAT FAITH IS NOT REALLY FAITH IF THERE IS NO RISK OR DOUBT AT ALL. FAITH IS NOT THE SAME AS CERTAINTY. WE CANNOT PROVE TO OTHERS THAT GOD EXISTS OR THAT HE LOVES US. WE CAN ONLY DISCOVER GOD'S LOVE FOR OURSELVES AS WE SEE GOD AT WORK IN OUR LIVES, AND EVEN THEN ONLY WHEN WE TRUST HIM TO SHOW US.

Doubting Thomas
Thomas was a believer but his faith was mixed with uncertainty. He could not believe Jesus was alive again unless he saw and touched the scars. The phrase "a doubting Thomas" has come to mean a person who refuses to believe something without proof.

❧ ABOUT THE STORY ❧

This story shows that even a close friend of Jesus could doubt what had actually happened. So the author stresses that those who believe today are in a way showing more faith than Thomas and the others. He is also making the point that there is plenty of evidence to convince us that it did happen – the evidence of the disciples written down for us and the generations of Christians since.

The Appearance at Galilee

SEVERAL of the disciples gathered one evening by the Sea of Galilee. The men looked out over the water at the beauty of the setting sun. They shared fond memories of all the precious times they had been on the lake with Jesus, floating in private in Peter's little boat, far from the crowds of disciples on the shore.

Now, once again, the ex-fisherman pushed his boat into the sea and his friends jumped in: James, John, Thomas and Nathaniel among them. They unfurled the sail and felt the wind push them into deeper waters. Under the stars, they cast their nets and sat quietly together, waiting.

All night long the men fished, but time and again they raised their nets to find them empty. There was still nothing in the nets by the time the dawn began to show itself over the glassy water.

"Have you caught anything?" came a voice, floating over the waves to the fishermen.

The disciples looked towards the shore and made out the small figure of a man on the beach.

"No! Nothing!" they hollered back.

The man cupped His hands to His mouth and called back, "Try casting your nets to the right of the boat!"

Peter and his friends decided they may as well try the stranger's advice. As they lowered the nets over the side, they felt them grow heavy with fish. In fact, it took all the disciples' combined effort to heave them back up again!

As John watched the hundreds of slippery bodies wriggling on the floor of the boat, he remembered a time when Jesus had given similar advice, and exactly the same thing had happened. Of course! he thought, turning to Peter and beaming broadly. "It's the Lord!" he cried.

At once, Peter's face lit up and he dived straight off the

❖ ABOUT THE STORY ❖

Just as Jesus was recognized by Cleopas on the road to Emmaus by a familiar action, so John recognizes Jesus in an action which is also very symbolic. When this had happened before, Jesus had called the fishermen brothers to be His disciples. It was as if He was calling them again to go out and be "fishers of men", to draw others into His kingdom. The special words for Peter were because Peter had let Jesus down by denying Him.

Jesus the shepherd
This statue of Jesus as the Good Shepherd comes from Turkey and dates from the 300SAD. Jesus saw Himself as a shepherd, with people as His flock. He said, "I am the good shepherd. The good shepherd lays down his life for His sheep. I know my sheep and my sheep know me".

Catching fish
In Jesus's time, people caught fish with nets, like the disciples in the story, or with a hook and line. The fish-hook shown here is made of bronze, but earlier ones were made from bone or iron. Fish were an important source of protein, as not many people ate much meat. Although fishermen often made a good living, they worked very hard. After fishing for most of the night, they then had to haul in the catch, mend the nets and sails, and dry, salt or pickle the fish ready to be taken to markets in other towns and villages.

boat into the water. Laughing with delight, the disciples watched as Peter splashed out for the shore in his eagerness to reach Jesus. Turning the sail into the wind, they headed for the beach themselves.

Peter ran dripping up the beach to find that Jesus was busy getting a little fire going.

"Go and bring some of the fish!" Jesus yelled. "Then come and have some breakfast!"

The overjoyed Peter immediately ran back down the shore to where his friends were landing the boat.

"Hurry up!" he yelled, practically jumping up and down with excitement.

Minutes later, together again with their master, Jesus's friends enjoyed the most delicious meal they had ever tasted, in the warmth of the early morning sun.

After they had all eaten their fill, Jesus turned to Peter and looked deep into his eyes.

"Peter," He asked, seriously, "do you love me?"

"Yes, Lord," the disciple replied, "of course I do!"

> ## Lord, you know everything, you know that I love you.

Jesus asked the question twice more. Each time, Peter grew more offended that Jesus felt He had to ask again. Peter didn't realize that each time he told Jesus he loved Him, his friend was forgiving him for having denied he knew Jesus on the night He was arrested.

At the third time of asking, Peter cried, "Lord, you know everything! You know very well that I love you!"

"I want you to look after my people like a shepherd looks after his flock," Jesus replied, "and follow me."

PETER'S EXPERIENCE TELLS PEOPLE TODAY THERE CAN ALWAYS BE A NEW START WITH JESUS WHEN WE LET HIM DOWN. HE DOES NOT FORSAKE US WHEN WE FAIL HIM. IT IS POSSIBLE TO WORK FOR HIM AGAIN.

Fishers of men

This picture shows Jesus speaking to the disciples as they fish from their boat. Jesus said, "Come, follow me and I will make you fishers of men." In this story, the disciples are actually fishing, but Jesus is telling them that by teaching others the ways of Christianity, they would be acting as fishermen of people.

The Ascension

FINALLY, it was time for Jesus to leave the world. He tenderly gathered His disciples together and walked with them once more to the Mount of Olives. It was there, among the groves in which the companions had walked and talked so often, that Jesus said His farewells.

"Don't leave Jerusalem yet," Jesus told His 11 friends. "For John baptized you all with water, but in a short while you will be visited by the Holy Spirit, who will baptize you again. With the powerful gifts my Father will send you, I want you to go and tell people about me through all nations of the world. Preach my gospel to the whole creation, to the very ends of the earth. Baptize all those who believe as my followers, in the name of the Father, and of the Son, and of the Holy Spirit, and teach them everything that I have taught you. For all those who believe and are baptized will be saved from their sins."

Jesus looked around at His friends' sad faces. He lifted up His hands and blessed them.

> ❝ *While He blessed them, He parted from them and was taken up into heaven.* ❞

"Don't forget," He said, softly. "I am with you always, even until the end of time."

As Jesus spoke, He was lifted up into a dazzling cloud of glory that blazed from up above and hid Him from the disciples' view. All at once, the cloud faded to a glimmer of light, and then it disappeared. Jesus was gone, and the disciples were left gazing up into the blue emptiness of the Jerusalem sky. Their minds were filled with awe and their

hearts were heavy with sorrow.

Voices from nearby brought the staring disciples back to earth with a bump.

"Men of Galilee," they said, "why do you stand looking up to heaven?"

The disciples shook themselves and looked round. They saw two strangers standing nearby in gleaming white robes.

"Jesus has gone from you and is now in heaven. But one day He will return, and He will be just the same as now, when you have seen Him go."

Overcome by wonder and strangely comforted, the disciples slowly made their way back to Jerusalem. In their heart of hearts, each man knew for sure that he wouldn't be seeing Jesus any more. Yet the friends also knew for certain that one day Jesus would return again in glory. After all, Jesus had proved that He never broke a promise, no matter how impossible it seemed.

Olives
In the story, Jesus walks with His disciples among the olive groves. Olives were one of the main crops of ancient Israel. Some fruit was eaten whole but most of the crop was pressed to extract the oil. Olive oil was used in cooking, in lamps and as a lotion to soothe the skin.

The Holy Trinity
Christians believe that there are three persons in God: the Father, the Son, or Jesus, and the Holy Spirit.

❧ ABOUT THE STORY ❧

This is the last resurrection appearance. The "ascension" of Jesus is an acted parable, a picture. It is supposed to make it clear to the disciples that Jesus is going where they cannot follow yet, to heaven. We use symbolic language in the same way. Heaven is not a place up in the sky. Heaven is a completely different form of existence to anything that we know or can experience on earth.

Christian Art Around the World

JESUS was crucified by the Romans, who ruled Israel at that time. He had been handed over to them by the Jewish priests, because of His refusal to submit to their authority. Although the Roman governor, Pontius Pilate, could not find Jesus guilty of any crime, he eventually bowed to pressure and sentenced Jesus to death.

The crucifixion took place outside Jerusalem, at the time of the Passover, just before the Sabbath. Jesus was 33 years old. Crucifixion was a common method of execution at that time, involving a slow, very painful and very public death. First, the Roman guards flogged Jesus and taunted Him, forcing Him to wear a crown of thorns on His head. After this, He was too weak to carry His own cross to the place of execution, so it was carried by a pilgrim called Simon of Cyrene. When He arrived at Golgotha, Jesus was stripped and nailed to the cross, where He died after about six hours.

Three days after the crucifixion, according to the Bible, Jesus rose from the dead just as He had promised He would. A group of women went to the tomb where His body had been buried and discovered it was empty. One of the women, Mary Magdalene, was the first person to see the risen Christ. Over a period of forty days, Jesus appeared to His disciples in Jerusalem and Galilee, and continued to teach them, just as He had done before His death. He commanded them to tell everyone the gospel, or "good news", that His death had made forgiveness and new life possible for all. Then He rose up, or "ascended", to heaven, returning to His Father.

Jesus's death is seen by Christians as the ultimate sacrifice. They believe that He gave his life to pay the price for all the sins of mankind. Because of the resurrection, Christians think of Jesus not as a dead hero, but as a living Saviour who has overcome death. They believe that He helps and guides those who follow Him and that, by offering them the chance of eternal life after death, He makes it possible for them to overcome sin and death, just as He did.

During the reign of Constantine, the first Roman Christian emperor (306–337), the cross became a symbol of Christianity. At first, the cross was empty, which symbolised Christ coming back to life. More recently, the crucifix has become more important. This is a cross with Jesus still on it. As a symbol, this emphasises how Jesus suffered for people's sins.

In the 1500s and 1600s Catholic missionaries, mainly from France, Spain and Portugal, travelled all over the world, spreading the Gospels to people who would not otherwise come into contact with Jesus and His teachings. This has meant that today, *Christian art* is found all over the world.

Mount of Olives, Jerusalem
This is a picture of Jesus chalked on the floor near the Mount of Olives, at the very heart of Christianity. It shows a heavenly, glowing Jesus before the cross. This emphasises Jesus's resurrection, and His promise of eternal life for all who believe in Him.

Guatemala
This lady is carrying a picture of Jesus as part of an Easter procession. Processions like this one, which recreate Jesus's walk with the cross to be crucified, happen in Christian communities all over the world at Easter. This one is in Guatemala, a small country in Central America.

Far Eastern Christianity

This shrine is in Tacloban City, in the Philippines. It is made up of carved, wooden images. Christ is in the centre. Around him are Matthew, Mark, Luke and John, who wrote the Gospels.

Crucifixion

This is the sort of scene of the crucifixion that is most often seen in Christian art. It shows Christ on the cross, and important people gathered around Him. On the left is a Roman centurion, and on the right of the picture are Mary Magdalene, Mary, mother of Jesus, and Salome.

Ethiopia

The strong history of Christianity in Ethiopia, in Africa, that is shown in this decorated altar piece, stems in part from the Bible story where the apostle Philip, baptizes an Ethiopian minister. Tradition in Ethiopia claims that this minister, who was probably a royal treasurer, was the first person to spread the Gospel in Ethiopia.

India

This is a painting of Jesus, held by children in the city of Madurai, in India. Most of the people in India are Hindu, but the first Christian missionaries arrived in the 1500s. A missionary is a religious person who travels around the world trying to convert people in other countries to their religion.

Faith in Peru

Peru is a country on the western coast of South America. It has a strong Christian tradition. The majority of the people are Roman Catholic. The first Catholic missionaries arrived in Peru in the 1500s.

The Gospels

THE word "gospel" literally means "good news". In the New Testament the gospel is the good news that God has fulfilled His promises to Israel by sending His Son, Jesus Christ, to save mankind. The first four books of the New Testament are known as the Gospels but, strictly speaking, they are four different accounts of the same gospel written by four early Christians.

Most of the material contained in the four Gospels would have been passed around by word of mouth before it was written down. The first person to spread the gospel was Jesus Himself. After His death, the disciples carried on teaching people about His life. As those people alive during Jesus's lifetime began to grow older and die, the need was felt for a written record of events. The four books known as the Gospels were written during the second half of the 1st century AD. Three of them – Matthew, Mark and Luke – contain common material although they present it in different ways. The fourth, John, stands apart from the others. Together the four books give a full picture of Jesus.

The first Gospel, Matthew, is presented in a very orderly way and has an emphasis on Jesus's teaching. It was traditionally believed that the author of the first Gospel was the disciple Matthew, but this view is no longer widely held.

Matthew includes most of the stories told in Mark, together with many sayings of Jesus and some other stories. He links the New Testament with the Old Testament much more closely than the other Gospels do, focusing on Jesus as the fulfilment of the prophecies about the coming of a Messiah. Matthew also describes the Christian church as 'the new Israel', explaining that because Jesus was rejected by so many of the Jews, Israel has been expanded to include non-Jews, or Gentiles. He stresses that whereas in Judaism it was the law that was supreme, in Christianity, it is Christ Himself.

The second Gospel, Mark, is usually thought to be the earliest. The author is traditionally believed to be John Mark of Jerusalem, a companion and interpreter of the disciple Peter. In fact, Mark's Gospel has sometimes been called Peter's Gospel, because the influence of the disciple is so apparent.

Mark is shorter and simpler than the other three Gospels, and there is a noticeable lack of detail. One explanation for this may be that Mark's Gospel has its roots in the oral tradition, word-of-mouth story-telling. When stories are repeated from

---

TIMELINE

JESUS, THE GOOD SHEPHERD

• Jesus turns and heads for Jerusalem.

AD33

JUDAS ACCEPTING HIS SILVER FOR BETRAYING JESUS

• Jesus enters Jerusalem on the back of a donkey, fulfilling the Old Testament prophecies of the Messiah.

• Jesus clears the temple of traders and money lenders.

THE LAST SUPPER

• Jesus and His disciples eat their Passover meal, The Last Supper. Jesus breaks the bread in the ceremony that becomes the Communion.

• The disciples go with Jesus to pray in the Garden of Gethsemane, on the Mount of Olives near Jerusalem.

JESUS IS FLOGGED BY THE ROMANS

memory, they become simplified. Mark's purpose in writing his Gospel was not to produce a work of literature, but to summarize the facts and communicate the truth. His Gospel is best understood as a written record of Peter's teaching.

The author of Luke, the third Gospel, was a well-educated man, with a knowledge of medicine. Through his close contact with Paul and other early Christian leaders, Luke had the opportunity to acquire first-hand knowledge about the life of Jesus and the history of the early Christian church. Luke's Gospel, like Matthew's, includes nearly all the material contained in Mark, but it has been rewritten in a more complex and professional style. It also includes much of the teaching of Jesus which is found in Matthew, together with other information. Luke also intends his Gospel to be seen as a historical work. He does not simply tell the stories but tries also to demonstrate their reliability. More than the other Gospels, Luke focuses on the human interest aspects, such as Jesus's concern for social outcasts. He also emphasizes Jesus's role as Saviour.

It is generally believed that the fourth Gospel was written by the disciple John, or at the very least by a disciple of John's, using his memoirs as a basis. This direct link to Jesus gives the book of John a special importance. John was probably the last Gospel to be written, and the author was likely to have been aware of the contents of the other three. However, the material contained in John is quite different. Unlike the other Gospels, it focuses less on incidents that took place at Galilee and more on Jerusalem. None of the parables are included, but John includes a lot of material that does not appear in the other Gospels. One significant difference is that Jesus often speaks in long dialogues unlike anything found in any of the other three Gospels.

John's Gospel is often seen as more of a personal interpretation of Jesus, rather than a straightforward account of His life. Instead of just telling the story of Jesus's life on earth, John brings out the meaning of it for his readers. His main purpose is to reveal the glory of Jesus as the Messiah, or Saviour, and the Son of God. His aim is to convert his readers to this belief and so to bring them into eternal life.

THE HOLY GRAIL

• Jesus is arrested in the garden.

• Peter is accused of being a follower and colleague of Jesus. He denies knowing Jesus, and the cock crows.

• Jesus is tried by Pontius Pilate. Although Pilate cannot find Him guilty of anything, He is condemned to death.

JESUS BEFORE THE SANHEDRIN

• Jesus is crucified. Christians believe he was dying for the sins of all the world's people.

THE HARROWING OF HELL

JESUS APPEARS AT GALILEE

• Jesus blesses the disciples, His friends and companions, and He ascends to Heaven to take His place by God.

AD33

Glossary

apostle
The group of twelve men that Jesus picked from His disciples were called apostles. They were the closest people to Him, and learned the most from Him. The group of apostles also includes Saul, who converted to Christianity after Jesus's death.

baptism
Jesus commanded that His followers be baptized to show they had been converted. Baptism involves immersing people in water. John the Baptist baptized many people as a sign of repentance and inner cleansing. The apostle Paul later said that Christian baptism is symbolic. When the person disappears beneath the water and then reappears, they are symbolically undergoing death, burial and resurrection, as Christ did.

disciples
As Jesus travelled round Galilee, teaching and preaching to the people there, people started to follow Him and His way of living. These people were called disciples. From the larger group of the disciples, Jesus chose his particularly close group of followers, called the apostles.

gentile
This is a general term for nations, and which came to mean anyone who is not Jewish. Jesus made sure that he preached His message to gentiles as well as Jews.

Gospel
Some of the people who followed Jesus's teaching recorded His life and works in writing. These are known as the Gospels, which means "good news". These writings have been passed down through the years and now form part of the New Testament. The Gospels are credited to Matthew, Mark, Luke and John.

kingdom of God
The kingdom of God is not an earthly kingdom. Jesus said that the kingdom of God is within everyone who follows His teachings, and tries to live their life in a Christian way.

Messiah
This means anointed one in Hebrew. The word Christ is the equivalent word in Greek. It means one chosen by God. By the time of Jesus, all the Jews were hoping for a great Messiah-king to set up an everlasting kingdom. Jesus's kingdom, the kingdom of God, was not an earthly kingdom. Jesus was not an emperor commanding armies as many were expecting. The kingdom of God will last forever.

ministry
Jesus spent about three years travelling around Judea, teaching the people about how they should live their lives and respect God. This is called His ministry.

miracle
Jesus performed many miracles during his ministry in Galilee, healing the sick and dying, casting out demons, and even bringing people back from the dead. Miracles are sometimes described as "mighty works", and they are performed through the power of God.

parable
Jesus told stories to people, called parables, to teach them about the kingdom of God. The stories used people and situations that his audience would be familiar with, which made the point of Jesus's story easier for people to remember and to understand.

Pharisee
A strict religious sect, the name Pharisee means "separated ones". They were generally ordinary people, not priests, who closely followed Jewish law. Sometimes they extended the ways that these laws were applied to make them even harder to follow. For example, when they said that people must not work on the Sabbath, they meant people could not walk more than about 1km from their house, they could not carry a heavy load or even light a fire in their house.

repentance
If a person repents, it means that they are truly sorry for their sins. Jesus forgave the sins of those people who came to Him and were genuinely sorry for what they had done. But it also means being determined to leave sin behind, trying not to sin at all in future.

resurrection
Three days after Jesus died on the cross, He came back to life, He was resurrected. This is the main and central point of the New Testament, and of Christianity.

Sadducees
These were a group of people smaller than the Pharisees, but more influential. Most of them were members of the family of priests. Most of the information that we have comes from their enemies so is not very reliable. We do know that they did not agree with the extensions of the law that the Pharisees tried to impose on people. This is why the Sadducees did not believe in life after death, as this is not mentioned in the Old Testament.

Samaritan
When the Promised Land was conquered by the Babylonians the Jews were taken away to live in Babylon, a period known as the Exile. The city of Samaria was filled with people from other lands, taken there by the Babylonians. These people were hated by the Jews after this time for taking the Jews' cities. Jesus makes sure that He demonstrates his concern for them, and shows that the kingdom of God is open to everyone by using the Samaritans in his stories.

synagogue
In Jesus's time Jews went to the synagogue to worship, just as they still do today. The synagogue also served as the school for local Jewish children.

Index

Page numbers in **bold** refer to illustrations